Living Right— Living Well

Paula Rodriguez

Tanglewood Publishing

Living Right—Living Well

By Paula Rodriguez

Copyright 2010 by Tanglewood Publishing

All rights reserved.
No part of this book
may be reproduced in
any form without written
permission from

Tanglewood Publishing
Clinton, Mississippi
800-241-4016

ISBN-13: 978-0-9793718-6-8

ISBN-10: 0-9793718-6-4

Cover Photo by Laura Rodriguez

Layout and Design by Sara Renick/Indigenous Images

Printed in the United States of America

VERY SPECIAL THANKS

AS WITH THE FIRST BOOK IN THIS SERIES, I WANT TO THANK MY EDITOR for this project, Amy Carter. I first met Amy when she was twelve or thirteen years old, and I was a friend of her mother. Amy has since earned a master's degree in English and is now a friend in her own right. She has been through every lesson and has not only answered all of the questions but also edited all of the written work. Amy, I'm learning a lot, but I still couldn't have done this without you.

For theological guidance, I once again turned to some of my many pastor friends. Each one gave me valuable advice and encouragement. I would like to thank my husband, Charlie Rodriguez, and also Os Barnes, Roger Collins, Ken Elliott, Simon Kistemaker, Paul Long, Don Malin, Mike Milton, Buck Mosal, David Sinclair, David Wakeland and Richard Wiman for helping me to make sure the comments in this study are theologically valid and in accordance with Scripture and the Westminster Standards.

TABLE OF CONTENTS

Introduction ix
The Westminster Confession and Catechisms xi
A Note to Women xiii
How to Use This Study xiv

Lesson 1—The Moral Law 1

Lesson 2—The Introduction:
  The Preface to the Ten Commandments 9

Lesson 3—The First Commandment:
  You shall have no other gods before me. 16

Lesson 4—The Second Commandment:
  You shall not make for yourself a carved image. 24

Lesson 5—The Third Commandment:
  You shall not take the name of the LORD your God in vain. ... 31

Lesson 6—The Fourth Commandment:
  Remember the Sabbath day, to keep it holy. 38

Lesson 7—The Fifth Commandment:
  Honor your father and your mother. 46

Lesson 8—The Sixth Commandment:
  You shall not murder. 53

Lesson 9—The Seventh Commandment:
  You shall not commit adultery. 61

Lesson 10—The Eighth Commandment:
  You shall not steal. 69

Lesson 11—The Ninth Commandment:
  You shall not bear false witness against your neighbor. 76

Lesson 12—The Tenth Commandment:
  You shall not covet. 83

About the Author 91

INTRODUCTION

THE *WESTMINSTER CONFESSION OF FAITH* AND THE SHORTER CATEchism which grew out of it are statements of doctrine, of what many people believe are the teachings of the Bible. We who were involving in writing this study believe that they contain the best summary of what God has revealed to us through His Word. We also believe that if a person understands these teachings, they will bring much peace and comfort to his or her life in Christ. But we do not believe that understanding all of this doctrine is necessary to salvation.

The truths contained in the Shorter Catechism cannot be understood unless a person first has come to a saving knowledge of Jesus Christ. These truths are spiritually understood; they do not make sense to the human mind without the guidance of the Holy Spirit. If you have not yet established a personal relationship with Jesus Christ, this might not be the right time for this study. If you choose to continue with it, please remember that salvation comes first, then very slowly, the understanding of the knowledge of God. This particular study considers the Ten Commandments. Although these commands are from God, and are still important for our daily lives, we cannot be saved simply by obeying these laws.

Neither is The Shorter Catechism or the *Westminster Confession of Faith* the gospel. The Gospel is very simple: "Believe in the Lord Jesus Christ, and you will be saved." This means that we must understand that we are sinners and have broken the law of God, and that therefore we deserve to be punished. But Christ, in His mercy, took on our sins and died in our place. If we accept His death as punishment for our sins and agree to live in obedience to Him, out of our love and gratitude to Him, we will live forever with Him in eternity. That is the Gospel. The Shorter Catechism seeks to teach believers the doctrine of what we call the Reformed faith.

That is where this study comes in. Our goal is that by entering into this study, you will gain a better understanding of the Ten Commandments, as they are explained in the *Westminster Confession of Faith* and the Larger and Shorter Catechisms.

There are some parts of the Shorter Catechism that are easy to understand and others that are very difficult. God leads each of us into understanding of this doctrine in our own time; so if there are things that seem too hard to take in, we encourage you to pray, search the Scripture, and then let God lead you in your own time as He directs. We also encourage you to be patient with others as they take their own individual journey through the mysteries of God's plan. Let God be God. He is much better at it than we are.

THE WESTMINSTER CONFESSION AND CATECHISMS

ON MAY 13, 1643, THE BRITISH PARLIAMENT ORGANIZED AN ASSEMBLY of ministers (or "divines") to create standards for a Church of England that would be reformed in worship, government, and doctrine. The Assembly comprised 151 members, including 30 laymen, chosen by Parliament to represent the counties, the universities, the House of Lords, and the House of Commons. Three were ministers of the Reformed Church of France, serving congregations in Canterbury and London. Twenty-eight did not attend, and twenty-one were appointed later to replace members who did not attend or who died during the proceedings.

The Westminster divines, mostly teachers and pastors of churches, were described by the Parliament as "learned, godly, and judicious." And they were. The Assembly's members were all Calvinists in theology; the main difference among them was in their views of church government and discipline. This resulted in a number of groups or parties—moderate Episcopalians (most of whom declined to attend out of loyalty to the king), Presbyterians (much the largest group), and Congregationalists.

The Assembly met at first in Westminster Abbey's imposing Henry VII Chapel. As the weather turned cooler, the divines were glad to move to the more comfortable Jerusalem Chamber. Every member took a vow to "maintain nothing in point of doctrine but what I believe to be most agreeable to the Word of God; nor in point of discipline, but what may make most for God's glory and the peace and good of his Church." The Assembly met every day except Saturday and Sunday, from nine o'clock until one or two. In the afternoons, the divines worked in committees. One of the rules guiding the deliberations required that "what any man undertakes to prove as necessary, he shall make good out of Scripture." The minutes and other reports of the Assembly's work reveal a strong commitment to this rule.

Much of the time of the Westminster divines was taken up with preaching and hearing sermons. Many hours were spent in corporate prayer and discussion concerning the lessons of God's providence. There were 1,163 numbered sessions of the Westminster Assembly, the last coming on February 22, 1649.

Over the course of five and a half years, during a time of political and religious chaos, the Westminster Assembly created five great documents of theological orthodoxy and ecclesiastical stability for the church in England, Ireland, and Scotland.

The Westminster Confession of Faith is the Assembly's most important work. Drawing on the richness of the creeds and confessions of church history, the Westminster divines summed up in thirty-three chapters "what man is to believe concerning God, and what duty God requires of man." The Westminster Assembly also produced two catechisms—"one more exact and comprehensive, another more easy and short for new beginners." The Larger Catechism was completed in October 1647, and The Shorter Catechism a month later.

The Westminster Confession has been translated into many languages and has shaped Reformed churches and thought throughout the world. Its biblical faithfulness has helped many to know "how we may glorify and enjoy" God.

—excerpted from David B. Calhoun.
"The Westminster Assembly."
The Confessions of Our Faith.
The Fortress Edition. 2007.
Used with permission.

A NOTE TO WOMEN

WHY DOES A WOMAN NEED TO KNOW ABOUT THE SHORTER CATEchism? Shouldn't we leave the doctrine up to the men of the church? Well, that depends on what you mean by doctrine and how you want it taught.

If by doctrine you mean the decisions about the official statements as to what a particular denomination believes, then, yes, many denominations believe that the Bible teaches that those decisions should be left up to the men. But there are denominations that include women in making those decisions. And although the Westminster Confession of Faith addresses this issue, the Shorter Catechism does not, so we will not address it in this discussion either. However, if by doctrine you mean the things we need to know and understand about God and Jesus Christ, then aren't these the things that we talk to our friends, family, and children about on a daily basis? I hope so. And how sad if our only answer to the questions of others is, "I don't know. You'll have to ask a man."

We certainly believe that women are intelligent enough to handle biblical doctrine, and we think God believes so too. There are plenty of examples in the Bible to indicate this. Timothy was reminded by Paul to continue in the teaching he received from his mother and grandmother. Priscilla and Aquila are mentioned together; they worked hand-in-hand in spreading the Gospel. Many other women are commended by Paul in his letters to other Christians.

So let's not for a minute think that we don't have a place in doctrine. As I was writing this, I began to wonder why, if women are so instrumental in teaching doctrine to others, are most of the commands to teach our children given to men? Of course, God has given the ultimate responsibility for the household to the husband and father. But also, because it comes naturally to women to teach their children, there is no need for God to command us to do so. Proverbs 1:8 admonishes, "Hear, my son, your father's instruction, and forsake not your mother's teaching." It is just assumed that mothers will teach their children. But we do need to be certain that we are doing it right. That is the purpose of this study.

HOW TO USE THIS STUDY

AS A TEACHER, I ALWAYS WANT MY STUDENTS TO BE PREPARED WHEN they come to class. I want them to be familiar with the material before they hear what I have to say about it.

That is the way I have approached this study. First, I want you to be familiar with the material. I want you to see for yourself what Scripture has to say about these doctrines. I have done that by giving you questions to answer related to each of the Catechism questions. After you have answered the questions, then read what I have to say. Test what I say against what you have read. Your discussions will be much richer if you have prepared each lesson.

Finally, many people like to memorize the Catechism questions and answers. That is not my purpose, but I am not opposed to it. It is much more important, however, to understand the truths of the words than to memorize the words themselves.

The Shorter Catechism questions and answers used in this study are from the Fortress Edition, which is a standard English edition. This edition seeks to maintain the original wording of the Confession and Catechisms as often as possible, while updating archaic or obsolete language to make it more understandable to the modern reader.

If you have questions about the doctrines contained in these studies, please ask your pastor about them. I would also be happy to discuss these things with you via email. My address is *paula.catechism@gmail.com*.

LESSON 1
THE MORAL LAW

Question 39: What is the duty that God requires of man?

Answer: The duty that God requires of man is obedience to His revealed will.

1. What blessings did God promise the Israelites for obeying His commandments?
   Read Deuteronomy 11:8-15

2. I Samuel 15:22 compares obedience to sacrifice. Which pleases God more? Why do you think this is true?
   Read I Samuel 15:3, 20-22

3. What does obedience to God involve?
   Read Micah 6:8, James 1:27

Question 40: What did God at first reveal to man for the rule of his obedience?

Answer: The rule that God at first revealed to man for his obedience was the moral law.

4. How does everyone know what God requires?
   Read Romans 2:14-15

5. What is meant by the term "moral law"?
   Read Exodus 15:26; Deuteronomy 13:18

Question 41: Where is the moral law found to be summarized?

Answer: The moral law is found summarized in the Ten Commandments.

6. Where and how were the Ten Commandments given to the people?
   Read Exodus 19:20-20:1

7. How did Moses receive the first tablets on which the Ten Commandments were written?
   Read Exodus 24:12, 32:16

8. What happened to the first tablets?
   Read Exodus 24:18; 32:1-19

9. How were the tablets replaced?
   Read Exodus 34: 1, 2, 28

Question 42: What is the sum of the Ten Commandments?

Answer: The sum of the Ten Commandments is: to love the Lord our God with all our heart, with all our soul, with all our strength, and with all our mind; and our neighbor as ourselves.

10. Where do we get the summary of the Ten Commandments?
    Read Matthew 22:37-40, Deuteronomy 6:5

11. Name two or three things that you consider to always be wrong.

12. Name two or three things that you have done that you would consider to be wrong.

LESSON 1
THE MORAL LAW

Catechism Questions 39, 40, 41, and 42

IS THERE SUCH A THING AS RIGHT AND WRONG? THAT MAY SEEM TO you to be a ridiculous question. Of course there is. Some things are right and some things are wrong. Everyone knows that. The problem is that everyone doesn't know it. In today's world, even the very idea of right and wrong is being questioned. More and more people live by the philosophy, "What is wrong for you may not be wrong for me."

But as Tim Keller points out in his book, *The Reason for God*, that philosophy really doesn't hold up. There are things that we object to other people doing, even if those things do not seem wrong to them. The terrorists who steered those planes into the World Trade Center towers thought they were doing the right thing, but I doubt that many of us would agree with them, or even support their right to have done what they did. And whether the perpetrators accept the fact or not, child abuse and child pornography are wrong.

But how do we know what is right and what is wrong? To determine right and wrong, there must be a standard. One standard is the law of the land. If something is against the law, it is wrong. That works some of the time. But does that therefore mean that if something is not against the law it is right? There are things that although legal, most of us would consider unethical. For example, corporate executives may lay off hundreds of workers while giving themselves million-dollar bonuses. That is completely legal. In my opinion, it is also completely wrong.

Behavior like that is not against the law of the land, but it is against God's law. It is a basic failure to treat others as you would want to be treated. God demands obedience from all of us, whether we accept His rule or fight against it. He promises blessings to those who obey Him. In the Old Testament passages, those were physical blessings, and He still gives those today. But He does not promise freedom from trouble. He does not promise prosperity for obeying His commands. He does promise to care for us and to see us through all of the difficult circumstances of life.

When my husband was in seminary, there was a period where we had ten dollars to last us through the next two weeks. We had absolutely no idea how we would make it. Then, for the first time, one of our church deacons asked how we were doing financially. We told him, and he promised to see what the church could do to help. Problem solved, right? We thought so too, but that is not how God worked it out. In fact, I don't even remember how it worked out. I only know that we survived that two weeks before we received any help from the church. Our church family did care, and they did help, but that's not what got us through those fourteen days. It was God alone. We did not go into debt and we did not go without meals.

Later in our seminary days, we received a very large gift and had the opportunity to share with others who were in need. We literally went from want to plenty, back and forth, during those years. But we saw how God provided through it all. Did the periods of want mean that we were less obedient? I don't think so. I think God was using those opportunities to show us that He can provide for us no matter what the outward circumstances may be, and that is a far greater blessing than a few dollars in the bank.

Obedience to God must come from the heart and not from outward appearance only. God is not impressed with how many times a week we go to church, read our Bible, pray, witness to others, or any other thing we may do in His name if it is not done for the right reason. Any of it that is done for our own glory is meaningless. Do you worry about whether people know if you have been to church? Then you are going for the wrong reason. Do you pride yourself on the number of people you have led to the Lord? Then you are witnessing for the wrong reason. God can still use you, but He may not be pleased with your attitude. Does it upset you if someone else gets credit for something you have done in the church? Why are you doing it—for your glory or for God's? If it is for God's glory, what does it matter who gets the credit?

Micah tells us that God requires three basic things of us—to act justly, to love mercy, and to walk humbly with our God. Justice means that we want everyone to get what he or she deserves. We do not want to see the innocent hurt or mistreated or put down in any way. We want to see the guilty punished and the innocent spared and we want the punishment to fit the crime. We become angry when we see the powerful in life taking advantage of the less fortunate, and when we have power, we try to make certain that we treat everyone fairly.

Mercy dictates that everyone does *not* get what he or she deserves. We certainly don't want what we deserve, which is an eternity in hell for the sins we have committed. We want mercy from God. Mercy allows us to forgive others for the wrongs they have committed against us and to treat them with compassion. Mercy calls us to care for those less fortunate than ourselves and to be kind to those around us. Mercy cares for the sick, the prisoners, the elderly, the homeless, the young, and the disabled. As James tells us, mercy cares for the widows and orphans—those with no one else to care for them. Without mercy, our world would be a cold, dark, unloving place to live.

I think it is interesting that we are told in the same verse to act justly and to love mercy. Justice must be tempered by mercy, but mercy must also be guided by justice. The two must work together. There are those who must pay for their crimes or misdeeds, and there are those who should be forgiven in mercy. How do we know which is which? By walking humbly with our God. Through the guidance of the Holy Spirit, we can know how to treat each of our fellow human beings. If we in our own arrogance think we have things figured out and under control, we will quickly find out that things are not quite as simple as we thought. If we humble ourselves and depend on God for guidance, we can make wise decisions which are pleasing to Him.

It is also important to realize that whether they believe in God or not, everyone has a basic concept of what God considers right and wrong. Paul tells us in Romans that everyone has a conscience that can guide him or her in that knowledge. Many people try to ignore their conscience in their desire to please themselves, but that does not mean that it is not there. As a student of communication, I have learned that the more stridently a person argues for a particular position, the more he or she is concerned about the opposing viewpoint. Think about that the next time you hear someone loudly proclaiming his or her right to live in a way that you know is not pleasing to God. The more arduously the person defends his or her position, the more he or she is afraid of the truth of the other side, the truth of God.

God tells us what is right and wrong in His eyes throughout the Bible, but His law is summed up in the Ten Commandments. These ten regulations cover the basic principles by which God wants us to live. They were given to us by God Himself, written by His own hand. They are rules to make our lives easier and more pleasant; they are not meant to be burdensome. If all of mankind were to follow these ten rules, there would be no need for police or military forces, or even a judicial system. We could truly have peace on earth.

God engraved these rules on stone tablets, so they could not fade or decay. They were meant to be permanent. He had to do it twice, though, because Moses broke the first set. Can you picture the scene? Moses has had an amazing, intense forty-day experience with God, and he comes down from the mountain to find that the Israelites have gotten tired of waiting for him. They didn't know what had happened to him, or why he was taking sooooo long on the mountain, so they took matters into their own hands. They decided they needed a god they could see, and they made a golden calf. But God cannot be represented by anything we can see or touch. In fact, His second commandment was that they should not make such an image.

So Moses was angry—really, really angry. And in his rage, he threw down the tablets that God Himself had carved out and engraved. He destroyed the golden calf, ground it up, scattered in on the water, and made the people drink the water. (Maybe that made them sick?) Anyway, he was furious. He wanted to make them pay. God was angry too, and He was ready to destroy the entire nation. What they had done was a terrible thing. But Moses interceded with God for them, and God spared most of them, although some were put to death.

But the tablets were gone. So this time God had Moses carve out new ones, and again God Himself engraved the words on the stones. These laws are permanent and are not to be changed or put away. We are still bound to obey these rules. They are not man's rules, but God's.

Christ summarized these laws for us very simply. "You shall love the Lord your God with all your heart and with all your soul and with all your mind," and "You shall love your neighbor as yourself." We are to love God with the totality of our being, with everything that is in us. And we are to love others and treat others as we would love and treat ourselves. In the next few studies, we will look at the introduction to the Ten Commandments, and then at each commandment individually to see exactly how God wants us to do this.

LESSON 2
THE INTRODUCTION:
THE PREFACE TO THE TEN COMMANDMENTS

Question 43: What is the preface to the Ten Commandments?

Answer: The preface to the Ten Commandments is in these words, "I am the LORD your God, who brought you out of the land of Egypt, out of the house of slavery,"

1. What was life like for the Israelites while in slavery in Egypt? Read Exodus 1:11-14

2. How did God bless the Israelites in spite of their slavery? Read Exodus 1:15-20

3. What kind of slavery are we all born under today? Read John 8:34; Romans 8:15

4. What is life like for us under this slavery?
   Read Romans 1:29-32; James 1:14-15; Hebrews 2:15

5. How does God bring us out of this slavery?
   Read John 8:36; Hebrews 9:15; I John 4:18; Philippians 4:6-7

Question 44: What does the preface to the Ten Commandments teach us?

Answer: The preface to the Ten Commandments teaches us that because God is the Lord, and our God and Redeemer, therefore we are bound to keep all His commandments.

6. Why does God have the right to give us commandments about how we are to live?
   Read Psalm 146:6, 10; Deuteronomy 32:6; Galatians 4:4-6

7. Does obedience to the commandments earn a person a place in heaven?
   Read Romans 3:20; Ephesians 2:8-9

8. What is the purpose of the law?
   Read Romans 3:20

9. What sins have you been convicted of through reading or hearing God's Word?

10. Why are we to obey God's commandments?
    Read I Peter 1:15-16; I John 5:3; Isaiah 48:17

11. How do we know that God knows what is best for us?
    Read Isaiah 40:28

12. What is the result of obeying God's commandments?
    Read Isaiah 48:17-18

LESSON 2
THE INTRODUCTION:
THE PREFACE TO THE TEN COMMANDMENTS

Catechism Questions 43 and 44

THE MEMORY OF SLAVERY IS A BIG ISSUE IN THE UNITED STATES. FOR too many years, a significant segment of the population was held in bondage by another group. But slavery did not begin in America. Ever since one group of people was strong enough to conquer another group, there have been slaves. And much of the time, slaves were mistreated. In the days of Joseph, the Israelites were an admired and respected people in Egypt. They were given good land and were allowed to live their lives in peace. As the years went by, though, the Egyptians became frightened at their numbers, and they were enslaved. Then they were treated cruelly; they were made to work at strenuous labor for long hours, but they still grew in numbers.

The Pharaoh finally ordered that all the baby boys be killed as soon as they were born, but the midwives did not obey this order. Amazingly, they were not punished by Pharaoh; they were rewarded by God for their righteousness. As the Hebrews increased even more, Pharaoh ordered that all baby boys be thrown into the Nile River. I have often heard that Moses' mother disobeyed this command, but that is not really the case. She did obey it; she threw Moses into the river. She just put him in a basket first. What a clever woman! She found a way to obey the law and still save her son's life. For this she was blessed by being allowed to nurse her son for the next few years. But the Israelites were still slaves and were still mistreated.

We can be thankful that in the United States we have ended this practice, even though it is still in existence in other parts of the world. It is illegal in our country for one person to own another person. But that does not mean that we have no slavery, because everyone in our country is born as a slave. We are not slaves to other people; we are slaves to sin. As slaves to sin, we are bound to do whatever our master wants us to do. We will lie, cheat, steal, dishonor others, refuse to honor God, hate, murder, etc. And the irony is, we think that we are free. We refuse to acknowledge our slavery. We think that we are doing what we want to do, that we are making our own decisions, that we are in control of our own lives. But in reality, all the time we are doing the work of the one who owns us.

There is in each of us a conscience that will let us know that we are doing wrong, but we will ignore it. We are bound to ignore it by virtue of our slavery to sin. We must obey our master. Even if we hear our conscience, we can easily rationalize our actions and ease what little guilt we may feel. We are doomed to live in this slavery until we die, and then we are doomed to face the punishment for our choices.

Even if we wanted to, we couldn't free ourselves. There is no way we can break the chains that hold us in captivity. In ancient times, it was possible for a slave to earn enough money to buy his or her freedom, but that is rarely true in cases of slavery today. A slave is not a paid employee; any money he or she earns goes to the master. Neither can we earn our freedom from slavery to sin. We certainly can't buy our way out. Nor can we do enough good deeds to earn our freedom. God tells us that all of our good deeds are worth nothing. Slaves cannot free themselves.

However, a slave can be set free by someone else. I have heard of several cases of people buying slaves in order to set them free. Someone would have to care a great deal about a slave to pay a large sum of money to buy his or her freedom. Imagine you are a slave. Your life is under the total control of someone else. For years you have to get up very early in the morning and work until late at night doing whatever you are told to do. You don't get days off. You can't leave the house without permission. You and your entire family are subject to the whims of your master. Even if you have a decent master, this is not a pleasant life. Now imagine that a man comes along, buys you and your family, and sets you free. You can now do what you want. What would you say to this man? After "Thank you!" wouldn't your next question be, "Isn't there anything I can do for you?"

Wouldn't you be willing to meet his requests? Not out of fear, but out of gratitude. You would be free not to, but you would probably do whatever he asked. Suppose he asked you to honor him and be kind to his children. Would you be willing to do that? Are you willing to do that for the one who has set you free?

We were all born as slaves, but if we have trusted Christ, then he has bought us and set us free. His death on the cross paid for our freedom. We no longer have to obey our sinful master. We can reject sin and its entanglements and we are free to live a better life. And to help us live that life to the fullest, God has given us rules, which Christ summed up into two: "Love the Lord your God with all your heart and with all your soul and with all your mind." And "Love your neighbor as yourself." In other words, honor and revere God and be kind to His children. We can never obey God's rules perfectly; the purpose of His laws is to show us what we are doing wrong and how we should be living.

So how do we know that these rules are in our best interest? How can we be sure that obeying these rules will bring us the best life possible? There are several reasons we can know this. First, we can know because the One who made the rules is the One who made us. He knows how we operate and what is likely to cause us problems. He knows how we interact together and how to make that work in the best way possible. He not only created our bodies, but also our minds, our emotions, and our personalities. He knows everything there is to know about us, so He knows how to make it work.

If a car manufacturer were to tell you that you must change the oil in your car every 3000 miles for that car to run at its peak efficiency, you would trust him. Why? Because he made the car and he knows how it works, or more importantly, what is likely to make it stop working. You have probably heard the saying, "Children don't come with instructions." But they do. We all have instructions. In the same way the car manufacturer gives us instructions for the upkeep of our car, the God who made us gives us instructions for the upkeep of our lives, and he knows what is likely to make our lives stop working pleasantly. If we would obey a lowly car manufacturer, we should certainly obey the God of the universe!

The second reason we can know that obeying these rules will work for our best is that God knows far more than we can ever know. He can see consequences to our actions that we can never see. We may not be able to see the harm that may come from our actions, but God can. How much more pleasant are our lives when we live according to our manufacturer's instructions! If we follow His plan, we will have peace in our hearts and righteousness in His sight. That is not to say that it will be easy, but He promises to be with us each step of the way.

LESSON 3
THE FIRST COMMANDMENT:
YOU SHALL HAVE NO OTHER GODS BEFORE ME.

Question 45: What is the First Commandment?

Answer: The First Commandments is, "You shall have no other gods before me."

Question 46: What is required in the First Commandment?

Answer: The First Commandment requires us to know and acknowledge God to be the only true God, and our God, and to worship and glorify Him accordingly.

1. When we accept that God is the only true God, what else are we obligated to do?
   Read Deuteronomy 26:17

2. How does God know if we are acknowledging Him as the only true God?
   Read I Chronicles 28:9; Psalm 139:2

3. How are we to worship the Lord?
   Read Psalm 29:2; 100:2; John 4:24; Romans 12:1; Hebrews 12:28

4. How are we to glorify the Lord?
   Read 1 Thessalonians 5:16-18; Acts 17:11; 2 John 6; 1 John 4:21

Question 47: What is forbidden in the First Commandment?

Answer: The First Commandment forbids the denying or not worshiping and glorifying, the true God as God, and our God, and the giving to any other of that worship and glory due to Him alone.

5. How does Scripture describe a person who denies God?
   Read Psalm 14:1

6. What happens to those who refuse to acknowledge and worship God?
   Read Romans 1:18-31

7. How can even Christians give worship and glory to something other than God alone?
   Read Colossians 3:5

8. What things are you worshiping other than God alone?

Question 48: What are we especially taught by the words, "before me," in the First Commandment?

Answer: These words, "before me," in the First Commandment teach us that God, who sees all things, takes notice of, and is much displeased with, the sin of having any other god.

9. How does God describe the worship of other gods?
   Read Deuteronomy 27:15; Jeremiah 32:34; I Kings 14:9

10. What is God's response to the worship of other gods?
    Read 2 Kings 22:17; Psalm 78:58

11. What does it mean that God is jealous?
    2 Corinthians 11:2-3; Deuteronomy 32:16

LESSON 3
THE FIRST COMMANDMENT: YOU SHALL HAVE NO OTHER GODS BEFORE ME.

Catechism Questions 45, 46, 47, and 48

"YOU SHALL HAVE NO OTHER GODS BEFORE ME." WHAT DOES THAT mean? I will get to the "no other gods" part in a while, but what does "before me" refer to? Merriam Webster's Online Dictionary gives three definitions for the word "before":

1. in a higher or more important position than <put quantity *before* quality>
2. preceding in time <just *before* noon>
3. in front of or in the presence of <speaking *before* the conference>.

Let's consider each of these definitions to see how well they fit the commandment.

First, the commandment could mean, "You shall have no other gods in a higher position than me." This would allow for the possibility of other gods, but only in a subordinate position to the God of the Bible. Is this what God meant? I don't think so. In Exodus 23:13, God instructs Israel, "Do not invoke the names of other gods; do not let them be heard on your lips." In Deuteronomy 17:2-5, we are told that if a man or woman worshiped another god, he or she was to be stoned to death. Finally, in 2 Kings 17:38, we read, "Do not forget the covenant I have made with you, and do not worship other gods." I think It is pretty clear that God does not allow the worship of any god other than Himself, whether that god is primary or secondary in our worship. So we can rule out definition number one.

Second, we could interpret the commandment as "You shall have no other gods earlier than me." In other words, until you worship me, you should worship no god at all. What this interpretation says is that the worship of any other god is wrong. If we do not know that we are to worship the true God, the worship of any other god is sinful. Actually, this is not exactly wrong, but it does not encompass the full meaning of the commandment.

And until we begin to worship the one true God, we are all guilty of breaking the commandment in this way.

Third, we could read the commandment as "You shall have no other gods in my presence." At first, this interpretation might seem to limit the commandment. Have any of you had a son who wanted a pet snake or a pet tarantula? Did any of you give in, with the stipulation, "Just don't bring it in where I can see it"? As long as it wasn't in your presence, you could ignore the fact that it was in your house. So as long as we don't bring other gods into God's presence, then we are okay, right? That is an unanswerable question, since everything in the entire universe is always in the presence of God. Wherever we go, whatever we do, we are always doing it before God. So it is impossible to worship other gods without worshiping them in His presence. I think this is the meaning of the commandment.

You may be thinking by now that this commandment is not relevant to you. People don't pray to idols anymore. We are more sophisticated than that now. But there are certainly religions that worship a different god than the God of the Bible. The true God exists as one God in three persons, which we call a Trinity—Father, Son, and Holy Spirit.[1] Any religion which fails to acknowledge any one of the persons of the Godhead is not worshiping the true God.

There are also still many religions that do incorporate idols into their worship. Many well-meaning folks have fallen for New Age mysticism and the belief in the power of crystals, pyramids, and other talismans. While not exactly idols, these forms of occult power are contrary to the worship of God. In Leviticus and Deuteronomy[2] we are told that divination, sorcery, witchcraft, and spiritism are detestable to the Lord.

But let's assume that you have not engaged in any of these practices. How might you have broken this commandment? My sister and I just had a conversation about an event that happened years ago, when I was sixteen and she was eleven. I had just bought a new peppermint-flavored lipstick. I thought it was really cool and asked her if she wanted to taste it. She bit off about half of it! She claims that I was being way too sensitive about that

---

1 Matthew 28:19
2 Leviticus 20:27; Deuteronomy 18:10-12

lipstick. I say that "taste" is very different from "eat." I was very upset about that lipstick! Now what does that have to do with the First Commandment? It says nothing about eating lipstick. It does, however, have a lot to say about my attitude toward that lipstick. How upset should I have been? How important was that lipstick? Depending on the degree of my distress, could my attitude have been bordering on worship?

Okay, worship of a lipstick is pretty silly, and I am fairly sure I was not worshiping the lipstick. But what about more important things? What about your home? Your job? Your spouse? Your children? George Robertson, in his study *More Grace, More Love*, says that we worship what we fear losing. In other words, whatever we fear losing the most is the thing we worship the most. Is your biggest fear that you might displease God or act unfaithfully toward Him? If not, then you are probably worshiping something else more than you are worshiping God. Is your biggest fear that you will lose your job, your spouse, or your children? Is your biggest fear that your looks will fade, that you will grow old? We can worship people, jobs, and even youth. Any of this would be a violation of this commandment.

In Colossians 3:5, we are told that greed is the same as idolatry. Why is that true? Because in our greed, our focus shifts from serving God to getting more of the thing or things we want. Those things become the objects of our worship. We may not pray to them or bow down to them, but we orient our lives around them. We give them the place in our lives that God should have and that He rightly deserves.

Our God, the only true God, is a jealous God. He wants the relationship with us that He deserves. He wants the worship that He is due. He wants first place in our lives. You may have been told that jealousy is a harmful emotion; and that is true if you are talking about jealousy in the sense of envy. But there are times when jealousy is healthy. A husband and wife should be jealous of their marriage. They should be angry if someone tries to interfere with that relationship. Marriage is meant to be "till death do us part." If anyone attempts to win the attention and affection of either the husband or the wife, the other spouse has the right, and perhaps even the obligation, to be jealous. This is the kind of jealousy that God has. His relationship with His people is precious. If someone or something else seeks to steal our affection away from Him, He is jealous for that relationship. I'm sure you can think of times in your own life when your first affection was for something or someone other than God.

So, you see, you probably have been worshiping something other than God. We all have; we have all broken Commandment One. Now what can we do about it? First, we can be grateful that God has provided salvation and forgiveness for us through Christ. In Ezekiel 37:23, God makes it clear that He forgives this sin specifically. No matter what you may have been worshiping in the past, God will help you to turn away from that and to worship Him and Him alone. So our second step is to begin to try to worship Him properly and to give Him the place in our lives that He deserves.

To do that requires that God take first priority in our lives. We must obey His Word and seek to live in a way that is pleasing to Him. We must worship Him in spirit and in truth, which means that we must study the Scriptures to understand what pleases Him in worship. We must live our lives in a way that is glorifying to God. Basically, that means that we must first and foremost be obedient to God and to His commands. Paul tells us in I Corinthians that we are to glorify God in our bodies and in our spirits.[3] According to Christ, this means that we should let men see our good works and glorify our Father in heaven.[4] We must look out for the "gods" that might lure us away from giving God the worship that He is rightfully due. In Colossians 3, Paul admonishes us to put to death such things as sexual immorality, impurity, lust, evil desires and greed; and to rid ourselves of all such things as anger, rage, malice, slander, filthy language, and lies. At the same time, he tells us to clothe ourselves with compassion, kindness, humility, gentleness and patience, and to bear with each other and forgive whatever grievances we may have against one another.

This is a tall order, and we can't do it all at once. This is the process of sanctification. Slowly, little by little, the Holy Spirit will enable us to accomplish more and more of this, although we will never perfect it in this lifetime. However, the more we accomplish, the more our lives will glorify God and the more others will see Him reflected in us.

---

3 I Corinthians 6:20
4 Matthew 5:16

The worship of God is serious business. It is more than attending church on Sunday. It is the total giving of our lives to His glory. It is giving Him first priority in every part of our lives. The wonderful fact for us is that the more we give our lives to Him, the more peace and joy we can experience.

LESSON 4
THE SECOND COMMANDMENT: YOU SHALL NOT MAKE FOR YOURSELF A CARVED IMAGE.

Question 49: Which is the Second Commandment?

Answer: The Second Commandment is, "You shall not make for yourself a carved image, or any likeness of anything that is in heaven above, or that is in the earth beneath, or that is in the water under the earth. You shall not bow down to them or serve them, for I the LORD your God am a jealous God, visiting the iniquity of the fathers on the children to the third and the fourth generation of those who hate me, but showing steadfast love to thousands of those who love me and keep my commandments."

1. Why is it impossible to represent God by an image? Read John 4:24

2. When Moses came down from the mountain with the Ten Commandments, what had the Israelites done that angered him so much? Read Exodus 32:7

3. What did Aaron tell the people they were doing when they sacrificed to the calf?
   Read Exodus 32:5-6

Question 50: What is required in the Second Commandment?

Answer: The Second Commandment requires the receiving, observing, and keeping pure and entire all such religious worship and ordinances as God has appointed in His Word.

4. How are we to worship God?
   Read John 4:24

5. What specifically should we do in worship?
   Read Acts 2:42; Ephesians 5:19; Malachi 3:10

6. For whom should we pray in our worship?
   Read 1 Timothy 2:1-2

Question 51: What is forbidden in the Second Commandment?

Answer: The Second Commandment forbids the worshiping of God by images, or any other way not appointed in His Word.

7. What does the worship of God by images involve?
   Read Isaiah 46:5-7

8. How can we create God in our own image without creating statues or pictures?
   Read Isaiah 29:13; Matthew 15:8-10

Question 52: What are the reasons attached to the Second Commandment?

Answer: The reasons attached to the Second Commandment are: God's sovereignty over us, His ownership in us, and the zeal He has for His own Worship.

9. Why does God have the right to tell us how to worship Him?
   Read Revelation 4:11

10. What should be our response to God in worship?
    Read Romans 12:1

LESSON 4
THE SECOND COMMANDMENT: YOU SHALL NOT MAKE FOR YOURSELF A CARVED IMAGE.

Catechism Questions 49, 50, 51, and 52

HAVE YOU EVER SEEN THAT PRINT OF THE PAINTING OF JESUS PRAYING in the Garden of Gethsemane? That print is everywhere. My grandmother had one in her sewing room. And in the little church where my husband preaches, a dear lady donated one for the front of the sanctuary. It was hanging there when he first came to the church. Oh, boy. What do you do? Confront the elders and tell them to take that picture down immediately? Give a series of sermons on idol worship and graven images? Or leave well enough alone?

He decided to leave it, at least for a while. After a time, he mentioned it in a session meeting. The decision was made to leave it there until the lady, who was by then quite elderly, passed on. It has now been replaced by a cross. But does it really even matter? What is the big deal about a picture of Jesus?

Well, first of all, that picture of Jesus probably doesn't look anything like Jesus really looked. If you go to a great art museum, you will see an astounding number of paintings of Jesus or of Mary and the infant Jesus. The interesting thing is that they all look like the people in the place and time that the artist lived. Modern artists are a little bit more in tune with the fact that styles of dress have changed, so they portray Jesus and Mary in more accurate clothing, but they still look like the people the artist lives around. Caucasian painters and sculptors make Him white; African painters and sculptors make Him black; Asians make Him Asian, etc. So in that picture, if I remember correctly, He has brown hair, white skin, and blue eyes.

Jesus lived in the Middle East. He would have fit in with the people He lived with; He would have looked Middle Eastern. I don't think I have ever seen a painting or sculpture with a Middle Eastern Jesus. So, the first thing wrong with most of our paintings and sculptures is that they are just wrong.

That may be the only thing wrong. It depends on our attitude toward the picture. If we are prone to worship or honor the picture in some special way, then we have a problem. Then we are using the picture as a worship image, and that is clearly forbidden in the Second Commandment. (For that matter, if we are using the cross that replaced it as an image to be worshiped, that is also forbidden.)

If you have taught young children, you know how valuable pictures can be to help them understand a story. When you are reading them a book, they always want to see the pictures. According to Dr. D. James Kennedy in his book, *Why the Ten Commandments Matter*, using pictures of Jesus for illustrative purposes is not what is forbidden in this commandment. God is not telling us not to create art depicting biblical stories, not even stories about Jesus. Jesus did take on a human body. That body lived and walked on earth and then was pierced and killed in payment for our sins. Dr. Kennedy says that we can use our art to depict those events.

What is forbidden is the worship of that art, or the worship of God through that art. There are still many forms of Christianity that use art forms as aids in worship. They may tell you that they are just using the statues or icons as symbols to point the worshipers to God, but isn't that exactly what Aaron did? He told the Israelites that they were to celebrate a festival to the Lord. The golden calf, at least in some ways, was a representation of God. But that was a lame excuse. God does not want to be represented by anything in our worship, because He cannot be represented by anything. He is Spirit, and He is far greater and more magnificent that any of His creation.

Dr. Kennedy likens this to having a really bad picture taken of yourself. Have you ever had that happen? When one of our daughters was in high school, she did not take good pictures. Her school pictures were pretty bad. And the worst part was that everyone kept trying to make her feel better by saying, "They're great. They look just like you." But she didn't want to look like that! Those people were not at all helpful. And the pictures did not look like her. Oh, sure, they looked like she looked for the split second when the picture was being taken, but they did not capture her vibrant personality or sense of humor. They were expressionless and empty. Just like those pictures did not accurately reflect my daughter, nothing that we could draw or paint or sculpt could come remotely close to reflecting the splendor and majesty of God Almighty. So we shouldn't even try.

It's not just through the use of physical objects that we can fail to worship God properly. In both the Old and the New Testaments, God confronts the religious teachers of the day for failing to worship Him properly. He says that they say the right words, but their hearts are far from Him. Instead of worshiping Him in the way He desires, they have made up their own rules for men to follow. How might that be visible in the Church today?

Well, what about the Shorter Catechism that we are studying right now? Or the *Westminster Confession of Faith*? How do you regard that document? If you consider it to be equal to the Bible, then you are guilty of breaking this commandment. These statements were written by godly men, and I truly believe that they are accurate and correct, but they are not, and do not claim to be, divinely inspired. They are not the Word of God.

I grew up in a church where I seldom, if ever, heard the Gospel preached. We were taught how to live nicely and to be kind to others, but I don't remember ever hearing about my need for a Savior. Of course, it could be that I just wasn't ready to hear that message, but I don't think that is the only reason I never heard about my need for Christ. After I became a Christian, I still attended that church for a while and I still did not hear the Gospel. I taught Vacation Church School (that's what they called it) during the summer, and our curriculum included only one Bible story for the entire week. The other stories were just made up by men.

I soon left that church for one that was much better. Several years later, while attending a Christian seminar, I ran into a couple who had both attended that same church. They were now also Christians, and the husband was attending a seminary in Dallas. When I returned home, I was talking with a friend and sharing my excitement that this couple had come to know the Lord, but my friend said, "But that seminary isn't Reformed." He couldn't share in the joy that they now loved the Lord because they didn't share his exact theology!

Folks, Reformed theology is not the Gospel. I believe it, but I can love those who don't. I can rejoice in those who come to know the Lord even if their theology is different from mine. Let's don't let our knowledge of doctrine put a stumbling block between ourselves and other Christians. Let's don't let rules or doctrine, even if they are the right rules and doctrine, separate us from loving our brothers and sisters in Christ.

If we are truly concerned about worshiping God in the proper manner, we will be serving Him with all our heart, with all our soul, with all our mind, and with all our strength. We will offer our bodies as living sacrifices to Him. If God is our focus, other things will fade in comparison. If there are things in your life that you are using as idols, get rid of them and ask for His forgiveness. Focus on God as He truly is. Give Him the glory and honor and worship He is due, in the way He commands it. He will gladly receive your worship, and you will be blessed in giving it.

5

LESSON 5
THE THIRD COMMANDMENT:
YOU SHALL NOT TAKE THE NAME OF THE LORD YOUR GOD IN VAIN.

Question 53: Which is the Third Commandment?

Answer: The Third Commandment is, "You shall not take the name of the LORD your God in vain, for the LORD will not hold him guiltless who takes His name in vain."

Question 54: What is required in the Third Commandment?

Answer: The Third Commandment requires the holy and reverent use of God's names, titles, attributes, ordinances, Word, and works.

1. What is God's name?
   Read Exodus 3:13-15

2. By what other names is God known?
   Read Exodus 15:3; 34:14; Psalm 92:1; Ezekiel 39:25; Amos 5:27; Matthew 1:21, 16:16; John 14:26

3. By what attributes or characteristics is God known?
   I Chronicles 16:35; Jeremiah 10:16; 23:6; 50:34; John 14:26: Romans 8:15

4. What name or names do you usually use for God?

5. What does it mean to "call on the name of the Lord"?
   Read Romans 10:9, 13; I Corinthians 1:2; Zechariah 13:9

6. When did people first begin to call on the name of the Lord?
   Read Genesis 4:26

Question 55: What is forbidden in the Third Commandment?

Answer: The Third Commandment forbids all profaning or abusing of anything by which God makes Himself known.

7. How are we to treat the name of the Lord?
   Read Deuteronomy 28:58-59; Psalm 68:4, 138:2; Malachi 1:11-14, 2:2

8. How can we profane or abuse God's name?
   Read Leviticus 24:11; Deuteronomy 5:11, 28:58; Malachi 1:14, 2:2

Question 56: What is the reason attached to the Third Commandment?

Answer: The reason attached to the Third Commandment is that, however those who break this commandment may escape punishment from men, yet the Lord our God will not allow them to escape His righteous judgment.

9. How much does God punish those who take His name in vain?
   Read Exodus 34:5-7

10. How have you misused the name of God?

LESSON 5
THE THIRD COMMANDMENT: YOU SHALL NOT TAKE THE NAME OF THE LORD YOUR GOD IN VAIN.

Catechism Questions 53, 54, 55, and 56

THE STORY I AM ABOUT TO TELL YOU IS TRUE. I HESITATED TO SHARE it, but I have decided that I need to. My husband was the pastor of a small church in a small town. The longer we served in that church, the more we became concerned about the spiritual well-being of some of the members, and even some of the church officers. Many of the church members seemed to be overly concerned about really trivial details of the church and not at all concerned about spiritual things. One Sunday evening a group of us were decorating the church for an upcoming event, and someone asked if we should move the large Bible from the communion table to make room for a floral arrangement. The basic décor of the church was in the hands of a few of the elderly women, and we were not sure they would approve of our moving the Bible. As we discussed the pros and cons, one woman in the group walked away and said, "Well, you can do what you want to, but I'm not touching that d____ Bible."

Are you shocked? I was speechless. This woman called herself a Christian; her husband was an elder in the church. I'm sure none of you would use such a term in connection with the Holy Bible. Or maybe some of you are not so shocked. Maybe you are thinking, "What's the big deal? It's just a book."

But it's not just a book; it is the living Word of God. Now I don't think the Bible is so "holy" that it should be kept in a special place, that only certain people should be allowed to read it, or that no one should desecrate its pages by writing in them. I have carried Bibles around and written in the pages until they were quite ragged-looking. That is using the Bible for the purpose that God intended—for study and for training in righteousness. But it is a special book because it was written by God Himself through the hands of specially chosen men.

So what does this have to do with taking the Lord's Name in vain? Only that everything about the Lord should be treated with reverence. According to the catechism, this includes His Name, His titles, His attributes, His ordinances, His Word, and His works.

God gave Himself many names and titles in the Bible. He is called I Am; The God of Abraham, Isaac, and Jacob; The Lord; The Lord Almighty; God Almighty; The Sovereign Lord; The Most High; Jesus Christ; The Holy Spirit, and the most unusual, Jealous. His attributes are many, but they include Savior, Redeemer, Our Righteousness, Portion of Jacob, Maker of all things, and Counselor. All of these names, and others you may find in Scripture, are to be used with utmost respect.

Does that mean you should never use phrases such as "Thank God!" Well, that depends on if you really mean it. If you are truly thanking God, then that phrase is appropriate and necessary. But if you are just using it as an expression of happiness, then no, it is inappropriate and actually sinful. Some folks throw around the Name of God so lightly, it is obvious that they are not thinking about God at all. We need to make sure we are never in that position.

I heard of a young man who, whenever he heard someone say "Jesus Christ!" in a profane way, would say "He's here. What did you need Him for?" I'm sure he upset a lot of people, but he got their attention! So many people just don't think about what they are saying.

In an interesting contrast, I was in a philosophy class with a young man who was a self-proclaimed atheist. As we were discussing arguments for or against the existence of God, this man would not even say the word "God." He always spelled it out: G-O-D. It is as if he were afraid that if he said the name, he would bring God into existence. Of course, I think he knew that there really is a God and it scared him to death. But he was very much aware of what he was saying. As an atheist, he showed more respect for the Name of God than many professing Christians do.

Many people, in an effort not to misuse the Name of God, use His attributes instead. For example, rather than say "Oh my God" they will say "Oh my goodness." But is this really any better? According to the Catechism, it is not. Goodness is an attribute of God; only He is totally good. To use His attributes in a profane way is also disrespectful and irreverent. So we all probably need to improve our vocabularies.

So is that it? As long as we don't say anything wrong, we are clear of breaking Commandment Three? Not so fast. Scripture gives us several other ways that we can be guilty of abusing the Name of God. In addition to what we say, we can abuse His Name by what we do or fail to do.

In Deuteronomy, Moses tells us that failure to obey God's laws is dishonoring to His Name. I could discuss this at length, but I won't. Let's just say that God makes it very clear throughout Scripture what He wants us to do and how He wants us to live. Every time we fall short of that, and we all fall short, we are sinning against Him and abusing His Name. We are failing to give Him the glory He deserves. By calling ourselves Christians, using His Name, and failing to live before others as He directs us to live, we are causing others to fail to glorify Him as well.

The prophet Malachi instructs us that by failing to give God His proper offering, we are dishonoring His Name. Whatever you believe the proper offering to be (many people believe that to be ten percent of your income), have you ever failed to give that amount to God? If so, you have profaned His Name. You have told Him that you were more important than He is, and that you could not trust Him to provide for you. Malachi also says that serving God for our own selfish purposes is an abuse of the Name of God. How many times do we do things for God or for the church hoping to receive recognition or reward?

So once again, we are guilty, guilty, guilty. This is getting old, isn't it? Let's face it. We are going to see that we have broken every one of the Ten Commandments. But we should have known that. John tells us in his first letter that if we say we have no sin, we are deceiving ourselves; but if we confess our sins, He is faithful to forgive our sins and to cleanse us from all unrighteousness. So what should we do about this sin? First, let's confess that we have misused God's Name and ask for His forgiveness. Then second, let's get things right. Let's treat God's Name, and everything associated with God, with respect and honor. Let's praise His Name, sing to His Name, rejoice in His Name, and fear His Name. But let's also call on His Name. As His children, we have that privilege. In one sense, to call on the Name of the Lord means to trust in Him for our salvation. This began in the earliest time of human existence, in the days of Adam and Eve and Seth. In another sense, to call on the Name of the Lord can mean to call on Him in times of trouble. As those who believe in Him, we can come to Him with every care and concern, because He is interested and involved in even the smallest aspect of our lives. This is our blessing as His chosen people.

LESSON 6
THE FOURTH COMMANDMENT:
REMEMBER THE SABBATH DAY, TO KEEP IT HOLY.

Question 57: Which is the Fourth Commandment?

Answer: The Fourth Commandment is, "Remember the Sabbath day, to keep it holy. Six days you shall labor, and do all your work, but the seventh day is a Sabbath to the LORD your God. On it you shall not do any work, you or your son, or your daughter, your male servant, or your female servant, or your livestock, or the sojourner who is within your gates. For in six days the LORD made heaven and earth, the sea, and all that is in them, and rested the seventh day. Therefore the LORD blessed the Sabbath day and made it holy."

1. What is to be done on the six days that are not the Sabbath?
   Read Exodus 20:9

2. What is the purpose of work?
   Read Proverbs 14:23; Ecclesiastes 3:22; Ephesians 4:28;
   I Thessalonians 4:11-12; 2 Thessalonians 3:7-9

3. What is God's attitude toward those who refuse to work?
   Read 2 Thessalonians 3:10

4. Who are we working for?
   Read Colossians 3:23

Question 58: What is required in the Fourth Commandment?

Answer: The Fourth Commandment requires the keeping holy to God such set times as He has appointed in His Word, expressly one whole day in seven, to be a holy Sabbath to Himself.

5. What was the Sabbath Day created for?
   Read Leviticus 23:3; Mark 2:27

Question 59: Which day of the seven has God appointed to be the weekly Sabbath?

Answer: From the beginning of the world to the resurrection of Christ, God appointed the seventh day of the week to be the weekly Sabbath; and the first day of the week ever since, to continue to the end of the world, which is the Christian Sabbath.

6. Why do we celebrate the Sabbath on the first day of the week?
   (What is the significance of the first day of the week?)
   Read Mark 16:2-6

Question 60: How is the Sabbath to be sanctified?

Answer: The Sabbath is to be sanctified by a holy resting all that day, even from such worldly employments and recreations as are lawful on other days; and spending the whole time in the public and private exercises of God's worship, except so much as is to be taken up in the works of necessity and mercy.

7. What kinds of things should be done on the Sabbath?
   Read Mark 3:1-5; Luke 23:55-56; Acts 17:2-3

Question 61: What is forbidden in the Fourth Commandment?

Answer: The Fourth Commandment forbids the omission, or careless performance, of the duties required, and the profaning the day by idleness, or doing that which is in itself sinful, or by unnecessary thoughts, words, or works, about our worldly employments or recreations.

8. What should we not do on the Sabbath?
   Read Hebrews 10:25; Leviticus 23:3

Question 62: What are the reasons attached to the Fourth Commandment?

Answer: The reasons attached to the Fourth Commandment are: God's allowing us six days of the week for our own employments, His establishment of a special ownership in the seventh, His own example, and His blessing the Sabbath day.

9. Who was the first person to observe a Sabbath day?
   Read Genesis 2:3

10. What do you usually do on the Sabbath?

11. Is there anything you feel you should change about your activities on the Sabbath?

LESSON 6
THE FOURTH COMMANDMENT: REMEMBER THE SABBATH DAY, TO KEEP IT HOLY.

Catechism Questions 57, 58, 59, 60, 61, and 62

I LOVE SUNDAYS. I LIKE GOING TO CHURCH, WORSHIPPING THE LORD, and seeing my friends. I also love the fact that I am commanded not to work. No matter what I see around the house that needs my attention, I am commanded by God to leave it until tomorrow. This is wonderful. I am by nature a Scarlet O'Hara kind of girl—"I'll think about it tomorrow; tomorrow is another day." This doesn't get me very far on most days, but it is exactly the right attitude for Sundays. On Sundays, God commands us to rest. He knows we need it, so He commands us to do it. Why are we so reluctant to take the gift He offers us?

Before we consider that question, though, I want to look at the first half of this commandment: six days you shall labor and do all your work. This is really a two-part commandment. We focus on the second half, but we can't ignore the first. God commands us to work. Work is the way we provide for ourselves and our families; God does not want us to be dependent on others. We should also work so that we have something to give to others. There are times when other people can't work, so we should try to have enough to share. In addition, honest work provides us with a good reputation in the community. It doesn't matter what your work is; if you do it diligently and honestly, others will recognize that and respect you for it.

We are also to enjoy our work. I have been especially blessed to have "stumbled" into a career that is extremely challenging and satisfying. Of course, I don't really think I stumbled into it at all; even though I had no idea what I was doing, God was directing me all along. My personality is split pretty evenly between extroversion and introversion; I love being with people, but I also need a significant amount of time to work alone. In my job as a college professor, I have a good balance of both. I get to work with students and other faculty, but then I get to work alone in my office as well. God has truly blessed me in this, and I am very grateful. If you have not been so fortunate, I would encourage you to think about what you really enjoy doing and see if you can make that an income-producing occupation. It might take some time or some additional education, but God intends that we find fulfillment and enjoyment in what we do. We have to do it for a lot of years, so it helps if we like it!

Whatever we are doing, though, we should be doing it for the Lord. Sometimes we may be tempted to do less than our best, but if we see ourselves as serving Christ, rather than our earthly employers, we will be less likely to act on that temptation. This is one thing I want to impress on my Christian students (especially the ones who make a show of their Christianity). As students, their job is to study. They should do this as though Christ were their instructor. Most of them are content just to get by. I don't think that's what Christ expects from them, or from us either.

So for six days, we are to work diligently. Then we get a day of rest. That is a tremendous gift. God actually tells us to stop. Stop striving, stop stressing, stop running around in circles. Just stop. Rest. Let it go for a while. Come to worship Him. Be inspired and invigorated in your faith. Remind yourself of what is really important and that God is there with you in whatever is going on in your life. Take time to read the Bible. Read an inspiring Christian book. Take a walk and be awed by God's creation. But rest from the labors of the other six days.

Some of you who have small children may find it difficult to rest. Children make the same demands on us on Sunday as they do on every other day of the week. Perhaps you could tuck away some special toys or videos, especially those related to your Christian faith, and let the children use those only on Sunday. While they play or watch the video, you can take a few minutes to rest. Or perhaps you can find an activity, such as taking a walk, which you find restful, but that can be done with the entire family. Read a good book to your children. The important thing is that this day be different, for your children as well as yourself.

Since my husband is a pastor, I want to say a word about pastors and other church workers. Of necessity, they have to work on the Sabbath. They must be there to preach and teach and to keep things going for the rest of us. But they need a day of rest as well. And it's not Saturday. Saturday is the day the entire family can be together and work as a family around the house. This is not a Sabbath for the pastor or church worker. He or she needs another day to truly rest. This is not just my opinion—it's God's opinion. We are all to have a Sabbath rest. God did it and so should we. If you are a church leader or have influence over one, make sure those who work for your church have their Sabbath as well.

So what are we allowed to do on the Sabbath, and what are we not allowed to do? Well, three things are clear: we are allowed to worship God on the Sabbath, we are allowed to do works of mercy on the Sabbath, and we are not allowed to do the work that we would do on the other six days of the week. That leaves a lot of gray area. Should we go out to a restaurant to eat? Should we watch movies? Should we travel? I have friends who believe that we should not do these things, and I have other friends who find no problem with them. How do we know who is right?

I wish I had a clear answer, a list of definite do's and don'ts, but Scripture doesn't give us one, so I certainly won't either. Here is what I do know. In Isaiah 58:13, we are told that we are not to do whatever we please or go our own way on the Sabbath. In 1 Corinthians 10, Paul tells us that all things are lawful for us, but not all things are profitable; and he says that we must do everything for the glory of God. In Romans 14, he explains that believers have different opinions about what is lawful and what is not, such as eating meat or treating one day differently from another. In such regards, if a person thinks something is sinful, but does it anyway, then he has sinned, because he did what he believed to be sinful. If another person does not think it is sinful, then he may do it and it is not sinful. It is the attitude of the heart that is important. If we do what we consider to be sinful, then we are telling the Lord that we are willing to break His law. But if we do not believe it to be sinful, then we believe that we are abiding by His law. However, Paul admonishes us neither to judge one another nor to put a stumbling block in one another's way.

So my interpretation of these passages would be that in those areas where Scripture is silent, each person or family must prayerfully decide what they should and should not do on the Sabbath. Then they should abide by that decision. If they have decided that a certain behavior is sinful, they should not do it. But they must not extend those rules to everyone. If Scripture is silent on an issue, we should not jump in and try to replace it with our own opinion. If a person or family has decided that a certain activity is not sinful, then they can feel free to do it. However, if they will be spending time with others who do consider it sinful, then they should refrain from doing it out of respect for their brothers and sisters in Christ. Remember that this only applies to those gray areas where Scripture does not give us clear direction.

Above all, the Sabbath is a gift from God. It was made for us to give us rest from our labors. It gives us time to focus on the truly important things in life: our relationship with God and with others. We so often want to ruin it by maintaining business as usual. We continue with our stress and worry and busyness, and then we wonder why we feel "burned out." There is seldom anything so important that it can't wait another day. The laundry and the dirty floors will still be there tomorrow. (Unfortunately.) Anything that has to be done can be done early with foresight and advance planning.

We are all guilty of using the Sabbath as just another day. We may go to church, but after that, we get back on the same merry-go-round of work and stress. God is ready and willing to forgive us for this. In Micah chapter 7, He says that He will pass over our rebellious acts and that rather than holding on to His anger, He will cast our sins into the depths of the sea. So again, let's confess that we have been guilty of misusing the Sabbath that God has provided for us. Then let's take His gift and use it as He intended. Enjoy the Sabbath. Worship. Rest. You know you need it and so does God; that's why He gave you a whole day to do it.

LESSON 7
THE FIFTH COMMANDMENT: HONOR YOUR FATHER AND YOUR MOTHER.

Question 63: Which is the Fifth Commandment?

Answer: The Fifth Commandment is, "Honor your father and your mother, that your days may be long in the land that the LORD your God is giving you."

Question 64: What is required in the Fifth Commandment?

Answer: The Fifth Commandment requires the preserving of the honor, and performing the duties, belonging to everyone in their various situations and relationships, as superiors, inferiors, or equals.

1. As children, what does honoring your father and mother involve? Read Ephesians 6:1

2. As adults, what does honoring our father and mother involve? Read Leviticus 19:3; Proverbs 1:8-9; Mark 7:8-13

Question 65: What is forbidden in the Fifth Commandment?

Answer: The Fifth Commandment forbids the neglecting of, or doing anything against, the honor and duty that belong to everyone in their various situations and relationships.

3. What types of things are we not to do regarding our father and mother?
   Read Exodus 21:15, 17; Proverbs 15:20,19:26

Question 66: What is the reason attached to the Fifth Commandment?

Answer: The reason attached to the Fifth Commandment is a promise of long life and prosperity (as far as it shall serve for God's glory, and their own good) to all who keep this commandment.

4. What is unusual about the Fifth Commandment?
   Read Ephesians 6:2-3

5. How does our relationship with our parents change with marriage?
   Read Genesis 2:24 or Matthew 19:5

6. Are there other times when we should leave our parents, physically or spiritually?
   Read Matthew 19:29

7. What place should our parents take on our priority list?
   Read Matthew 10:37

8. How are we to deal with elderly parents?
   Read Proverbs 23:22; 1 Timothy 5:1-2

9. Does this apply to our own parents only or to all of our elders?
   Read 1 Timothy 5:1-2 again

10. What things do you need to change regarding your treatment of or attitude toward your father and mother?

LESSON 7
THE FIFTH COMMANDMENT:
HONOR YOUR FATHER AND YOUR MOTHER.

Catechism Questions 63, 64, 65, and 66

MISSIONARIES AND PARENTS HAVE A SIMILAR CAREER GOAL—TO WORK themselves out of a job. Missionaries are trying to establish churches that national Christians can then take over and support on their own. Parents are seeking to raise children who can be independent and productive adults. Some of you who are reading this are both a parent and a child. Some of you are parents, but have lost your own parents. Some of you are children and have no children of your own. Some have lost your own parents but have no children. There is a place for all of you in this study.

The Fifth Commandment tells us to honor our father and mother. We are going to explore exactly what that does and does not mean. But before proceeding any further, we need to remember that much of this applies on a larger scale than just our immediate family. All of the elderly are to be treated in some respects as our parents. Most of the provisions attached to this commandment apply to everyone with whom you have a relationship, whether they are related to you or not.

First, how do we honor our parents? As children, we honor them by our obedience. Our parents were given to us by God to guide and direct us until we were old enough to navigate this world on our own. However, this stipulation does have an ending point. I do not believe we are called upon to obey our parents for our entire lives. That is fairly obvious for those who get married. Scripture makes it very clear that when a man and woman marry, they become one flesh. They form a new family. They leave their father and mother. This doesn't mean that they never see them again, but it does mean that they are no longer under their authority.

What about adults who have not married? Are they still bound to be obedient to their parents? This is just my opinion, but I think that when a person reaches the age that they begin to seriously contemplate marriage, or the age of financial independence, then they should be independent of their parents. They should become a new family of one.

Many parents have a hard time with this. They still want their son to be "mommy's little boy" or their daughter to be "daddy's little girl." I don't think this is a healthy relationship. Adult children need to be treated as adults and given the respect and independence that we would give our friends. If they ask for advice, give it. Otherwise, stay out of it. A young woman I know said that when she was in the hospital after giving birth to her first child, her mother-in-law came to her house and rearranged and redecorated it completely. This is way out of line! I don't care if this young woman has the worst decorating sense in the world [and she doesn't], it is her house. If you would not do something in a friend's home, don't do it in your children's. And if you would do things like that in your friend's home, then call me. We need to have a long talk.

So we honor our parents by our obedience only up to a certain age. After that, what should we do? We need to continue to respect them, listen to their instruction, and provide for them when they are older. We all know how to treat people with respect, but too often we fail to do that within families. We know each other's quirks and frailties so very well, and it is easy to make jokes of these. Do you laugh at the "stupid" things your mother has done? Do you joke about your father's lack of handyman skills? Is this respect? We can so easily hurt the feelings of others without meaning to and without their letting us know what we have done.

We also need to listen to the advice and instruction of those older and wiser than we are. People learn a lot through experience. Listening to advice can save us a lot of heartaches and headaches. That is not to say that our parents are always right and that we must always do what they advise. But we should at least listen and consider their opinion. They may not know all the facts or have all the knowledge they need, but before we write them off completely, see what they do have to say. They may be wiser and smarter than you think. If not, what did it cost you but a little time?

When our parents are elderly, we need to be sure their needs are taken care of. In today's world, that usually does not mean that we must provide for them monetarily, although sometimes it might. It might mean that we need to become our parents' advisors in making wise financial decisions. As people live longer, more of the elderly become easy prey for those who would take advantage of them. Just recently, I got my first email from Africa.

A Mrs. Edith Matthews said that her husband had died, and she had some money that she needed to get transferred into the United States. If I would just send X number of dollars, she could open a U. S. bank account, etc., etc. Have you been on Mrs. Matthews' mailing list? This is a familiar email scam to most of us, but some of our elderly parents are not as Internet savvy and are more trusting of others. As their children, we need to help protect them against those who would harm them for their own financial gain.

Does honoring our parents mean that they must take first place in our lives? Absolutely not. That place is reserved for God. We must never put anyone in the place He deserves. If we are married, our spouse must come before our parents as well. Hopefully, you will never have to choose between God and your parents, but some people do. Some people leave their parents, families, and everything to follow Christ. Those of us in the church must become their family. Others are called to leave their homes to serve God far away. Sometimes parents can try to stand in the way of their going. If you find yourself faced with such a dilemma, consider your parents' reasons for their objection. Seek godly counsel. And pray for clear direction from God. You may find that you are still called to go. Our parents cannot stand between us and doing the will of God.

And I want to add a note to the parents here—don't be those parents. If your child is called to serve God far away, especially overseas, rejoice in that. It will not be the easiest thing you have ever done in your life, but you will be greatly blessed. We've been there and done it—we even have the T-shirts! The first time my two older daughters took a plane to a mission trip destination, I literally panicked. During the time they were at their mission site, a plane crashed nearby. I was a basket case. I am not exaggerating. I had friends coming to my house to counsel with me and pray with me. My friend Judy put a rubber band around her wrist to remind her to pray for me. My girls were gone for a week and I thought I wouldn't make it. When we went to the airport to pick them up, Judy and I stood together waiting for the plane. As we saw the plane approaching, the rubber band on her wrist popped off and flew across the hallway. Judy said, "Well, I guess I don't need to pray for you any more."

As I am writing this, my two younger daughters are both overseas and my oldest daughter is planning to go in a couple of weeks. Before they leave,

I pray with them, give them a kiss, tell them I love them, and send them on their way. I sleep soundly that night. Did I do this on my own? Are you kidding! God has done a transforming work in me because He wants my kids overseas, and He doesn't want me to be a hindrance to them.

Yes, we are commanded by God to honor our parents. But as parents, let's be the type of parents that are easy to honor. If you have difficult parents, respect and honor them in spite of that. If you have young children, teach them obedience, and set the example by honoring your own parents. If you have adult children, treat them with the respect that you want from them. God promises blessings if you do.

LESSON 8
THE SIXTH COMMANDMENT: YOU SHALL NOT MURDER.

Question 67: Which is the Sixth Commandment?
Answer: The Sixth Commandment is, "You shall not murder."

1. Summarizing what you read in these verses, what is the definition of "murder"?
   Read Numbers 35:16-21

2. Summarizing what you read in these verses, is the accidental killing of another person considered murder?
   Read Numbers 35:22-24

3. Is killing other people in a righteous war considered murder?
   Read Joshua 8:1, 24

4. Is executing a person who is guilty of a crime considered murder?
   Read Exodus 21:14; Leviticus 20:2

5. When does a person become a person?
   Read Jeremiah 1:5

Question 68: What is required in the Sixth Commandment?

Answer: The Sixth Commandment requires all lawful endeavors to preserve our own lives, and the lives of others.

6. How should a person treat his or her own body?
   Read Ephesians 5:29

7. How should we protect the lives of others?
   Read Matthew 25:34-36; Proverbs 31:8; Joshua 2:1-6

Question 69: What is forbidden in the Sixth Commandment?

Answer: The Sixth Commandment forbids the taking away of our own lives or the lives of our neighbors unjustly, or whatever tends to do so.

8. How does the Bible describe our body?
   Read I Corinthians 6:19-20

9. Is it possible to commit murder in our thoughts?
   Read Matthew 5:21-22

10. How should we treat the elderly among us?
    Read Leviticus 19:32; 1 Timothy 5:1-2, 4, 16

11. How should we treat the disabled among us?
    Read Job 29:11-15; Luke 14:12-14

12. What instances can you think of where you have committed murder in your words or thoughts?

LESSON 8
THE SIXTH COMMANDMENT: YOU SHALL NOT MURDER.

Catechism Questions 67, 68, and 69

AFTER MY GRANDFATHER DIED, MY GRANDMOTHER MOVED IN WITH my mother. It was not a good match. They had very different ideas about how to do a lot of things. As my grandmother got older and more forgetful, it got worse. Those little things that Mother could have put up with on an occasional visit were hard to deal with on a day to day basis. One weekend they were visiting our house and my mother and I were having a conversation in the kitchen. My grandmother came in and asked us a question that she had already asked several times before, but that was getting fairly normal by this time. After she left the room, my mother turned to me and said, "If I ever get like that, just shoot me."

Have you ever felt like that? Just shoot me. Or just shoot them? We all have; of course, we don't mean it, any more than my mother did. We get exasperated and say things we don't mean. However, Jesus tells us that even saying things in anger is a sin like murder. But some people not only say it, they do it. And most of the time they go to prison. We know that it is very wrong to take a human life, no matter how irritating that life may be. It seems pretty clear, but where do we draw the line? Is killing another person always wrong? If not, when is it not wrong? When does the prohibition against murder begin to apply? What about taking one's own life? What about the terminally ill, the disabled, or the unwanted? Let's look at all of these cases.

First, is it always wrong to take another life? The answer from the Bible is clearly "no." There are times when taking a life is justified and even commanded. In times of war, lives will be lost. War is not a nice thing. It is not glorious. It is horrible in every sense of the word. But sometimes it is necessary. As Edmund Burke said, "All that's necessary for the forces of evil to win in the world is for enough good men to do nothing." Sometimes those good men have to go to war against the forces of evil. And some on each side will die. It isn't pleasant to think about, and no one wants it to happen; but there are times when we have to do it anyway.

There are also certain crimes that are so evil that God commands that those who commit them be put to death. Think of serial murderers such as Jeffrey Dahmer, Ted Bundy, John Wayne Gacy, and Charles Manson. These men showed no respect for human life and by their own actions, they convicted themselves of crimes worthy of death. Some of them were actually sentenced to death and some were not. But according to the Bible, they all deserved the death penalty. For the government to execute a person who has been found guilty of such a crime beyond the shadow of a doubt is not wrong. Personally, I think we need to be very careful before imposing such a punishment so that we don't execute innocent people, but in some cases the evidence is so overwhelming that there is simply no doubt as to who committed the crimes.

So not all killing is murder. But any intentional killing of an innocent human being is murder; so when does the prohibition against murder begin to apply? When does a person become a person? According to God, we become a person before we are born. Most scientists who are Christians believe that occurs at the moment of conception. At the precise instant that two cells unite to become one new cell, a genetically new individual is created. This one cell has its own unique DNA and will soon grow to become a recognizable and distinct individual. In week 5 of its development, its heart will begin to beat. In week 6, the basic facial features will begin to form. In week 8, it will develop fingers and toes, eyelids, ears, the upper lip and the nose. By week 9, hair follicles appear and many internal organs are forming. By week 10, its bones are forming. By week 12, its gender is obvious and it has fingernails and toenails.[5] But if its mother doesn't want it, a doctor can legally go into the womb, rip it apart and throw it away. Is this the deliberate killing of an innocent human being? I don't see how we can call it anything else.

But what if the baby is not whole, if there is something seriously wrong? What if the child will be mentally retarded or severely disabled? I would challenge you to ask a parent of such a child how they feel about parenting that child. Almost all of those I have talked to speak of the joy they have received from their children. Yes, their life is not the same as they dreamed

---

5 MayoClinic.com

it would be; but for many, it is actually better. But even if not, let me ask you about another scenario—suppose you have a healthy, perfectly normal child who is seriously disabled as the result of an accident. What would you do? Would you have a doctor come in and kill that child because your life was now going to be different from what you had expected? I hope and expect that your answer would be "Of course not!" You would love that child and do whatever was in your power to make his or her life a good one. So what's the difference? Whether there is a problem before birth or after birth, the child deserves to be loved and nurtured because he or she, just like all the rest of us, is created in the image of God.

What about those who want to die? Why is killing yourself considered wrong? Because, as I just said, God considers each of us to be precious. We are all made in His image, and He has a purpose for each of us. He intends for us to nourish and take care of our bodies. We may fight against that purpose, or life may impose unbelievably difficult circumstances on us, but that does not mean that He wants us to give up. God is always with us, no matter what the circumstances. All we have to do is call on Him; He promises that He will never turn us away.[6] We need to reach out to those who are in distress and who are in severe pain; perhaps our laws need to be changed to offer a greater variety of medical help to those who are suffering from terminal illness. When my sister's mother-in-law was dying of cancer, her doctor acknowledged that many families have resorted to buying heroin illegally to relieve the suffering of their loved ones. Maybe we should reconsider whether drugs such as this should be available for doctors to use for the terminally ill. Our compassion should be as great as it can possibly be, but only God should decide when life is over.

There is always the danger that society can cross over the line between a person's choosing to end his or her own life and society's choosing when his or her life should end. When we accept that death is an acceptable solution when our life is painful or unhappy or unproductive, then it is not too far to the next step of society's deciding that the elderly or the disabled are too much of a drain on society and that they should be "allowed" to "end their lives with dignity." What might begin as an attempt to allow the vol-

---

6 John 6:37

untary ending of one's life to relieve pain and suffering may become the expected action to take when we become too old or infirm to "contribute productively to society." I don't know what society views as productive, but as far as I am concerned, there are lots of ways to be of use to others.

My father's mother lived to be 103 years old. At the age of ninety, she started wondering why God was keeping her on earth. She was a strong Christian and she was ready to go home. I told her He was keeping her here for us, her children and grandchildren. She was an amazing inspiration to me, and through me she is an inspiration to my children. She was not earning any money, or able to do much work to help others physically, but she was a great joy and an emotional encouragement to all who knew her. Is that "contributing productively"? I think so, but I don't know how society as a whole would view it. I hope I never have to find out.

So as long as we are not involved in the taking of a life, we can breathe a sigh of relief on the sixth commandment, right? Not so fast. Remember back at the beginning of this lesson when I said that saying things in anger is a sin like murder? Well, have you ever done that? In Ephesians, Paul tells us to get rid of bitterness, rage, anger, brawling, slander, and malice;[7] in Colossians he adds filthy language to the list.[8] James says that our anger does not bring about the righteous life that God desires us to live.[9] When we harbor bitterness and anger in our hearts, we are also guilty of the sin of murder. We are desiring evil, or even death, for the person against whom we are angry. And we are only hurting ourselves in the process. In teaching us to pray, Jesus used the phrase, "Forgive us our debts as we forgive our debtors." And when Peter asked Him how many times we are to forgive a person for the same offense, Jesus told Him not to add to the number of times he guessed we should forgive, but to multiply. We are to continue to forgive others, not so much for their benefit as for our own. To refuse to do that, to store up resentment and anger in our hearts, is to be guilty of breaking this commandment. So once again, we are all guilty.

But once again, praise the Lord, there is forgiveness if we ask for it. Whether we have broken this commandment through our words, or even

---

[7] Ephesians 4:31
[8] Colossians 3:8
[9] James 1:20

committed the actual act, God can still forgive. James tells us in chapter 4 that if we draw near to God, He will draw near to us. He says that if we humble ourselves before the Lord, then He will exalt us. Even a heinous sin like murder can be forgiven by God.

All of life is meaningful to God. He created all of it, and expects us to honor and preserve it in thought and in deed. The taking of human life is necessary at times, but only when it is determined by law and cannot be avoided. We should treat every human being with the dignity and respect he or she is due as a person made in the image of God. In doing this, we can live with the peace of knowing that our hearts are right before others and before God.

LESSON 9
THE SEVENTH COMMANDMENT: YOU SHALL NOT COMMIT ADULTERY.

Question 70: Which is the Seventh Commandment?
Answer: The Seventh Commandment is, "You shall not commit adultery."

1. What is the meaning of the word "adultery"?
   Read Leviticus 20:10; Hebrews 13:4

Question 71: What is required in the Seventh Commandment?
Answer: The Seventh Commandment requires the preservation of our own and our neighbor's chastity, in heart, speech, and behavior.

2. Is it possible to commit adultery even if a person never cheats on his or her spouse?
   Read Matthew 19:9; Mark 10:11-12

3. What is God's plan for marriage?
   Read Genesis 2:24; Mark 10:6-8

4. How many wives are church leaders supposed to have?
   Read 1Timothy 3:12; Titus 1:6

5. What does Jesus say is an acceptable reason for divorce?
   Read Matthew 19:9

6. What reason does Paul add as an acceptable reason for divorce?
   Read 1 Corinthians 7:12-15

Question 72: What is forbidden in the Seventh Commandment?

Answer: The Seventh Commandment forbids all unchaste thoughts, words, and actions.

7. Is it possible to commit adultery in our thoughts?
   Read Matthew 5:27-28

8. How can you commit adultery in your speech?
   Read Ephesians 5:3-4

9. What does God have to say about sex before marriage?
   Read 1 Corinthians 7:1-2, 8-9; Ephesians 5:3

10. What does God have to say about sex within marriage?
    Read 1 Corinthians 7:3-5

11. In what ways could you change your behavior or speech to avoid the sin of adultery?

LESSON 9
THE SEVENTH COMMANDMENT: YOU SHALL NOT COMMIT ADULTERY.
Catechism Questions 70, 71, and 72

I WARNED YOU WAY BACK IN LESSON FIVE THAT WE WOULD FIND OUT that we have broken all of the commandments, but some of you thought you were safe on this one, didn't you? You have never cheated on your spouse, so you were sure you have never committed adultery. I hope you see after answering the questions that it's not so simple.

We would all probably like to work with a really narrow definition of the word "adultery." In fact, Dictionary.com gives as its definition of the word "voluntary sexual intercourse between a married person and someone other than his or her lawful spouse." If that were God's definition, most of us could rest easy here. But that is man's definition, not God's. Included in God's definition are all kinds of sexual immorality, including our thoughts, words, and behavior towards everyone we meet.

Let's start with behavior, since that's the most obvious. Why is God so opposed to adultery? Well, can you think of three good things that come out of an act of adultery? [I will give you two: the two people involved have a few moments of pleasure.] But there is no third good thing. Every other result is negative. Those two "good" things that I gave you aren't even really good because the people involved do not have lasting benefits; they are usually caught up in a tangle of lies and deceit and probably guilt. So those few moments of pleasure end up causing many more moments of discomfort and even pain. And what about the other people involved. The spouses of the people involved feel nothing but pain, as do the children, if there are children and they find out.

I saw a movie once where a husband cheated on his wife. In response, the wife took all of his belongings and put them in his car. Then she poured gasoline all over the car and set it on fire. This seems to me to be a completely understandable reaction. It is not something you should do, of course, but I can appreciate why you would want to. Adultery takes something precious between a husband and wife and throws it in the garbage. The pain it causes the innocent spouse can be almost unbearable. In fact, Jesus doesn't even ask the spouse who has been sinned against to continue to live with the adulterer; He says that this is a legitimate reason to dissolve the marriage. Anyone, including a pastor, who would advise a person to tolerate this kind of behavior is not giving biblical advice.

But suppose there are no spouses. Suppose the two people involved are single and simply want to enjoy each other physically. What could be wrong with that? The problem is that God did not wire us that way emotionally. We are made to join together with another person and to become one with that person. The marriage act is the ultimate form of that union. When we give ourselves to a person, we have invested some of our emotional energy into that relationship. Even for a brief time, we have become one with that person. How many times can a person do that without severe emotional impact?

And the consequences are not only emotional, they are also physical. According to the American Social Health Association, over 65 million people in the United States have some form of sexually transmitted disease. Each year, one in four teens contracts an STD. About half of all hepatitis B infections are transmitted sexually. ASHA estimates that one in five Americans has genital herpes, but that 90% of those people are not aware that they have the disease. The Centers for Disease Control revealed in 2008 that 26% of American girls aged 14-19 have at least one of the four most common types of STDs.

How can we avoid these horrible diseases? By remaining abstinent until marriage. We have all heard that the way around these STDs and unwanted pregnancies is "safe sex," but the failure rate for "safe sex" is anywhere from 2% to 20%. I think that even the conservative 2% failure rate is too high. That would mean that the method would fail once in every fifty sexual encounters. If you knew that once in every fifty flights a plane would crash, would you fly? Or if every fiftieth driver were certain to be involved in a serious accident, would you be afraid to drive? In the paragraph above, you can see the results of taking the chance on having even protected sex outside of marriage.

I cannot leave our discussion of sexual behavior without discussing relationships between people of the same gender. Although such behavior has always existed, it seems that it has become more open and more widespread in this generation. What did God have to say about it? In the Old Testament, these acts were considered capital crimes, punishable by death.[10] In the New Testament, Romans 1:26-27 calls these acts unnatural, shameful, indecent, and perversions. There are those who want to excuse this behavior on the basis that it is genetic, that a person is born with a predisposition to homosexuality, and that he or she cannot control the behavior. I am not sure that this is the case, but even if it were, how does society view other genetic conditions?

Let's look at one other type of condition, that of addiction. *The Handbook of Addictive Disorders* lists the following as mental health disorders: chemical dependency, workaholism, compulsive gambling, eating disorders, sex addiction, and compulsive buying. It is commonly accepted that addictive disorders have a strong genetic component; people are born with a tendency to engage in these behaviors. But how does society view this? Do we simply tolerate these behaviors and expect others to view them as acceptable lifestyle choices. Of course not. The subtitle of the above-mentioned book is *A Practical Guide to Diagnosis and Treatment*. We expect people with a predisposition to addictive behavior to get treatment for their behavior so that it does not continue. We do not condone the behavior because it has a genetic component.

We should look at alternative sexual preferences in the same way. No matter what the cause, these are unacceptable in God's eyes. And just like addictive behaviors, they need to be dealt with. If a person is an alcoholic, the best thing for her to do is to avoid alcohol and places where alcohol is served. If a person is a compulsive gambler, the best thing to do is to avoid people and places that promote gambling behavior. Likewise, if a person has a tendency toward homosexual behavior, it would seem to me that the best thing for that person to do would be to avoid people and places that promote that lifestyle. Remaining celibate is an honorable choice for many people; there are lots of single people in the world, some with heterosexual and some with homosexual tendencies. They can avoid much of the emotional and physical pain that comes with extra-marital sex by making that choice.

---

10 Leviticus 20:13
11 Matthew 20:21

How do we know that this commandment was not just culturally based? Perhaps our society has evolved to a point where sex outside of marriage is no longer frowned upon as it once was. Maybe this rule was given to or made up by a very restrictive society. Well, if the commandment had been written two hundred years ago, I would see your point. But it was given four thousand years ago. And in many of the cultures of the time, sex outside of marriage was practiced in their religion. Both male and female temple prostitutes are mentioned in the Old Testament. So far from being a restrictive society, the world of the Old Testament was probably more open to extramarital sex even than our society is today. Yet God forbids it.

The obvious conclusion is that God knows what is best for us. He did not give us rules to punish us or to make our lives miserable, but to keep us safe and happy. God is not opposed to sex; He created it. He is very much in favor of it in the proper context of marriage. He even gave consideration to women's enjoyment of the sexual union, which is something not found in most other ancient religious texts. In other ancient religions, women were not given much regard when it came to sexual matters (or any other matters). In the brief reading I have done, it appears that the Buddha gave instructions only to men when it came to sexual matters. The Hindu religion regarded the wife as the property of the husband, to the point of burning her alive on his funeral pyre. Yet the Bible gives as much consideration to the wife as it does to the husband in the sexual relationship. How progressive!

It is pretty clear that the rules for our sexual behavior have been given for our protection, with due concern for our enjoyment of sex within the context of marriage. Let's widen the scope of our attention now to our thoughts and our words.

Jesus makes it crystal clear that even thinking about someone in a lustful way is a form of adultery. It is not the same as committing the behavior, but it is adultery nonetheless. Now think of all the ways that society encourages this type of behavior. How many advertisements have you seen that entice the viewer through sexual images? And it seems that almost every movie made today has one or more sexually charged scenes. The world does its best to draw us all in to its lifestyle. And it works. My husband and I know of several ministers who have been drawn in and who have left their wives and families for another woman. We all need to be very careful; no one is above temptation.

In addition to our thoughts, we need to watch our words. The Bible warns us about obscene talk and coarse joking for a reason. Jesus warns us that the things that come out of the mouth come from the heart, including sexually immoral speech. If we are speaking in such a way, then we are thinking in such a way. And all of it is sinful.

In our day and time, sexual purity is seen as prudery. Both men and women flaunt their bodies to attract the opposite sex. Living together outside of marriage has become the norm; many languages have words to describe unmarried couples. I am not saying that we should sit in judgment of those who behave in such a manner. As Jesus said, "Let he who is without sin cast the first stone." Violating this commandment is no worse than violating any of the other nine.

Everyone has sinned, and as we have seen in this lesson, everyone has broken the seventh commandment. As with all sins, adultery can be forgiven. In Paul's first letter to the Corinthians, he says that no one who indulges in adulterous behavior can inherit the kingdom of God; but he adds that if we are cleansed by the blood of Christ, we can be justified before God. No matter what we have done, God is ready to receive anyone who calls on Him. Those who do not know Christ do not need us to condemn their behavior; they need us to lovingly lead them to the Savior. Accept others where they are and point them to Christ, while making sure that you are living a life that is in all ways glorifying to Him. Watch your thoughts, your words, and your actions to keep yourself pure. You will be blessed if you do.

LESSON 10
THE EIGHTH COMMANDMENT:
YOU SHALL NOT STEAL.

Question 73: Which is the Eighth Commandment?
Answer: The Eighth Commandment is, "You shall not steal."

1. How can we steal from our neighbor?
   Read Leviticus 19:13; Job 24:2

2. How can we steal from our employers?
   Read Titus 2: 9-10

3. How can we steal from the less fortunate?
   Read Deuteronomy 24:14-17; Isaiah 10:12

4. How can we steal from God?
   Read Proverbs 3:9; Malachi 3:8, 1:14

Question 74: What is required in the Eighth Commandment?

Answer: The Eighth Commandment requires that we utilize only lawful means in obtaining and furthering the wealth and outward estate of ourselves and others.

5. How should we acquire whatever wealth we may acquire?
   Read Proverbs 10:4; Psalm 112:1-3; Proverbs 3:13-16

6. What is the danger of trusting in wealth?
   Read Proverbs 27:24; I Timothy 6:7; Matthew 6:19

7. What should we trust in rather than riches?
   Read Philippians 4:19

8. What should be our request of God concerning wealth?
   Read Proverbs 30:7-9

Question 75: What is forbidden in the Eighth Commandment?

Answer: The Eighth Commandment forbids whatever does, or may, unjustly hinder our own, or our neighbor's, wealth or outward estate.

9. How can we correct our actions in regard to this commandment?
   Read Ephesians 4:28

10. Where should our treasure be?
    Read Matthew 6:20

11. In what ways have you been stealing from God or your fellow man?

LESSON 10
THE EIGHTH COMMANDMENT: YOU SHALL NOT STEAL.

Catechism Questions 73, 74, and 75

AS I WRITE THIS LESSON, THE ECONOMY OF OUR COUNTRY IS IN A shambles. I don't know if it will get worse or better. There is gloom and doom in every economic report I read or hear. What has gone wrong? Well, part of the problem is that a lot of people have broken the Tenth Commandment, but I'll get to that later. Another part of the problem is that some major players in the financial game have broken this one. People are willing to take other people's money in order to make themselves richer. And eventually it all comes crashing down. When people invest in a house of cards, it will eventually collapse.

Theft is a horrible thing, and there are so many ways to do it. The most obvious is simply to take what belongs to someone else. If you have ever had your house burglarized or your car or even your purse stolen, you know how traumatic it can be. On her first day of a visit overseas, my friend Ann had her purse stolen, including her passport. We had to spend over half of the next day at the embassy getting the passport replaced. The thief stole not only the objects in the purse, but our time as well. Objects can be replaced, but the time cannot.

Sometimes even objects can't be replaced. I have an heirloom ring that was given to me by my father-in-law. This is a very special ring to me because of the history behind it. My father-in-law, whom we called "D," had told my husband that when he wanted to get married, if D approved of his choice of a wife, he could have the ring for an engagement ring. Because they had very different value systems, my husband-to-be was not going to allow his father to have veto power over his choice of a wife, so he did not even ask for the ring. Several years later, D gave it to me anyway. Either he approved of me or realized he wasn't going to get rid of me, but either way, I felt accepted into the family. So I now have the ring. I have had it insured so that if it gets lost or stolen I can replace it. But I can't really replace it; I can buy a new ring, but it won't be the one D gave me.

I'm sure you wouldn't even think of breaking into someone's home or car and stealing things. But there are so many other ways to steal. What about at work? When we are at work, we are supposed to be doing work. How often have you made personal phone calls or sent personal emails on company time? In effect, you are being paid to make those calls or send those emails. Or have you ever "borrowed" office supplies to use at home?

In my line of work, I often have to deal with two other types of theft. In a 1998 poll by *Who's Who Among American High School Students,* 80% of the nation's best high school students admitted to cheating. According to *U. S. News and World Report,* 75% of college students admit to cheating, and 85% of college students think cheating is necessary to get ahead. Cheating on tests is nothing but theft of the work of other students. In other words, I will not try to prepare for the exam; I will let you work and prepare, and then I will steal your answers.

Another rampant type of theft is plagiarism, copying someone else's work and passing it off as your own. There are actually websites that encourage this. [There are also websites that can help instructors catch it!] In my department we teach public speaking and we require the students to turn in outlines of their speeches. Another professor told me about a student in her class who turned in a perfect outline. It was indeed perfect, because it was the exact outline that this professor had handed out as a sample outline in a previous semester! Sometimes plagiarism is pretty easy to catch! Parents and teachers must begin early to teach our children that stealing the work of others is exactly that—stealing.

Many otherwise law-abiding citizens steal from the government every year by cheating on their income tax. According to the Internal Revenue Service, the "tax gap" for tax year 2001, tax that should have been paid but was not, totaled $345 billion. Of that amount the IRS. estimates that it will eventually recover only $55 billion. I realize that we do not all approve of the ways that our money is used by the government. But what did Jesus say about taxes? When asked specifically whether we should pay taxes, He told us to give to Caesar what is Caesar's.[11] In other words, yes. Pay your taxes.

---

12 Galatians 1:10; 1 Thessalonians 2:4

I'm absolutely certain that Christ did not approve of everything that was done by the Roman government or by the Jewish leaders at the time, but still He paid the taxes He owed. We should do no less. To fail to pay taxes is to steal from those God has put in authority over us.

We can also steal from those who are less fortunate by failing to help them in their need, and by depriving them of their rights. Before we judge others, let's be certain of all of our facts; or better yet, let's not judge others at all. We are often quick to stereotype those on government assistance, but often we don't have the full story, or even half of the story. It actually should be the job of the church to help these people, but we have fallen down on the job, and the government has stepped in to do what we should have been doing. So let's be cautious about criticizing the government for doing what ought to be our job.

And finally, we can steal from God Himself. Whatever you believe the tithe should be, and many people believe that it should be ten percent of your entire salary, you should be giving that to the Lord in some form. Not to do that is to say two things to God: 1) I am not grateful for what You have given me and done for me, and I don't feel that I owe You anything, and 2) I don't trust You to provide for my needs and I feel that I have to do it myself. If you want to provide for yourself, God will let you, but He has more resources at His disposal than you do, so you are missing out on the riches that are available to Him.

So is wealth wrong? Not intrinsically, no. God does provide wealth to some people. Money is not the root of all evil, the love of money is. My husband and I have a friend who is very wealthy but who gives thousands of dollars a year to the work of various missionaries and missions agencies. He has been blessed, and he uses his blessings to bless others. To meet him, you would not know he was wealthy. He is not pretentious in the least. He is a really good business man and has a knack for investments, and God has blessed his talent. But he in turn uses his talent for God.

Which do you love more, God or money? Remember the story of the rich young ruler. When he asked Jesus what he needed to do to inherit eternal life, Jesus told him that the one thing he needed to do was to sell all of his possessions and give the proceeds to the poor. He couldn't do it. Jesus had found his weakness, the one thing he loved more than God.

What would you do with wealth if you had it? Buy more stuff for yourself? Give more to others? The prayer of Proverbs is a good one for all of us because the writer is asking for just enough—not so much that he will forget that it all comes from God and not so little that he will be tempted to steal to provide for his family. If we have just enough, then we can be content.

So what if you have realized that you have been stealing? Then stop. Do diligent work. Be honest in all your dealings. Give to those in need. Give to God. In Malachi 3:10, God actually invites us to test Him in the act of giving to see if He will bless us when we give to Him. It may be that God will give you wealth. If He gives it to you and allows you to enjoy it, that is a blessing from Him. Use it wisely. It may be that He will give you just enough. If you have enough, can you be content?

11

LESSON 11
THE NINTH COMMANDMENT: YOU SHALL NOT BEAR FALSE WITNESS AGAINST YOUR NEIGHBOR.

Question 76: Which is the Ninth Commandment?

Answer: The Ninth Commandment is, "You shall not bear false witness against your neighbor."

1. How does God deal with those who testify falsely against others?
   Read Proverbs 19: 5, 9

2. Other than giving false testimony, what other types of dishonesty in legal proceedings are we warned against?
   Read Exodus 23:1, 7

Question 77: What is required in the Ninth Commandment?

Answer: The Ninth Commandment requires the maintaining and promoting of truth between man and man, and of our own and our neighbor's good name, especially in testifying as witnesses.

3. How are we to speak to others?
   Read Ephesians 4:25; 1 Thessalonians 5:11, 14

Question 78: What is forbidden in the Ninth Commandment?

Answer: The Ninth Commandment forbids whatever is prejudicial to truth, or injurious to our own or our neighbor's good name.

4. How does God feel about those who tell lies?
   Read Psalm 5:6; Proverbs 6:16-19

5. Who is the father of lies?
   Read John 8:44

6. In what ways can we lie?
   Read Psalm 12:2; Ezekiel 13:8; Micah 6:11

7. What happens if a ruler is influenced by lies?
   Read Proverbs 29:12; Psalm 62:4

8. Why are we misled by lies?
   Read Jeremiah 5:30-31; Hosea 7:3

9. What does the Bible have to say about those who teach false doctrine?
   Read Psalm 78:35-37; Matthew 7:15; 1 Timothy 6:3-4

10. How did Rahab lie to the authorities over her?
    Read Joshua 2:1-16

11. What was God's response to this lie?
    Read Matthew 1:5; Hebrews 11:31; James 2:25

12. If God detests liars, why do you think He considered Rahab to be righteous because of her lie?

LESSON 11
THE NINTH COMMANDMENT: YOU SHALL NOT BEAR FALSE WITNESS AGAINST YOUR NEIGHBOR.

Catechism Questions 76, 77, and 78

DO YOU WANT TO BE LIED TO? THINK ABOUT YOUR ANSWER. OUR first response is, "Of course not," but perhaps there are times when we wouldn't mind a little white lie. What is the correct answer to the question, "Does this make me look fat?" Every husband knows, or ought to know, that the correct answer is always "No." Whether it's the truth or not, that's the answer. When a woman asks that question, she is not asking for the truth; she is asking for reassurance that she is attractive.

So how are we to interpret the Ninth Commandment? There are those who argue that this commandment means that we are to speak the truth in all circumstances and let God handle the consequences. Then there are those who say that although the truth is to be preferred, it is our reason for withholding the truth that is at stake, and that there may be good reasons, even godly reasons, for lying. I will tell you right now that my opinion lies with the second group.

First of all, the commandment is specifically addressed to lying in court, as a witness in a legal proceeding. We are always to tell the truth in that situation. Interestingly, we are not told here not to bear false witness in favor of our neighbor, but I would hesitate to do that for practical reasons. For example, if your neighbor is accused of a crime, and you testify that he was at home when you know he was not, you may be helping a criminal to go free. You may be a part of perpetrating that crime on the next victim.

But the commandment specifically warns us against testifying falsely against our neighbor. God tells us that He will not let those actions go unpunished. Not only are we not to testify falsely against someone, we are not to have anything to do with false charges or putting an innocent person to death. I am not opposed to the death penalty, but if I were to serve on a jury in a capital case, I would have to know beyond a shadow of a doubt that the accused person was guilty before I could sentence him or her to die.

So is that it? As long as we don't lie in court, we haven't broken this commandment? Not so fast. Even though the commandment addresses honesty in the courtroom, God tells us how He feels about honesty in our daily lives. God says that He hates liars; they are detestable to Him. We are to put off falsehood and speak the truth to our neighbor. So we are back to the question that began this lesson. Are we supposed to tell the truth all the time, every time, no matter the consequences? I still don't think so.

Look at the example of Rahab. Rahab was a prostitute—not a very godly occupation—in the city of Jericho. When the two Israelite spies entered the city, she hid them and told their pursuers that yes, the spies had been there, but that they had gone away at dusk. After the gates of the city had been closed, she helped the spies escape and told them how to avoid being captured. There is no way around the fact that Rahab told an outright lie to the soldiers who were pursuing the spies. So what was God's response to this? He blessed her and her family: first, by not killing them when Jericho was destroyed by the Israelites; second, by considering her actions to be righteous; and third, by giving her a place in the ancestry of Jesus Christ and honoring her by listing her name in His genealogy.

Clearly, this was a lie; and clearly, God was not opposed to it. What is the difference? What makes one lie sinful and another lie righteous? I think it has to do with the attitude of the heart. In my field of communication, we study lying. It is after all a form of communication. There are basically seven reasons for lying: to save face, to avoid tension or conflict, to guide social interaction, to expand or reduce relationships, to gain power, to benefit the listener, or to benefit a third party. Let's examine each one of these to see how God might view them.

First, lying to save face, or to save ourselves from embarrassment. "The check is in the mail." Who is benefiting from this lie? Only the person who is lying. We all want to look good in the eyes of others, so when we are afraid we might look bad, we lie to cover up our shortcomings. Paul warns us in his letter to the Galatians[12] and his first letter to the Thessalonians that we should be trying to please God rather than men. If this is our motive for lying, I think it's safe to say that God would not approve.

Second, lying to avoid tension or conflict. "I'm not upset; I just need to readjust to the change in plans." Again, what is our motive? Why do we not want to admit our true feelings? Couldn't we say, "Sure, I'm a little upset, but I'll readjust and it will be okay"? God does tell us that as much as it is within our power that we should live at peace with others. But I think most of the time we can do that and still tell the truth. When we lie for this reason, we are still more concerned about our image with other people than our obedience to God.

Third, lying to guide social interaction. "I have been meaning to call you." Once again, aren't we concerned about how we appear to others? What could we say instead? How about, "How have you been? It's been such a long time since I've seen you." Why lie?

Fourth, lying to expand or reduce relationships. "You're going downtown? Me too. Can I give you a ride?" or "I'd love to see you, but my schedule is really packed this week." This one gets a little tricky. We often lie at the beginning of a relationship because we aren't sure how the other person feels about us. It's hard to say, "I'm really kind of interested in you and I am willing to go completely out of my way in order to spend time with you. Hop in." I don't think this is a type of lie that we need to be concerned about, especially if the aim is to reduce discomfort for the other person involved. In the second example, though, we need to be careful about giving false impressions. Sometimes the truth, although it may hurt, is the best in the long run.

Fifth, lying to gain power. "If elected, I will _____." Enough said. This is always wrong. Always.

Sixth, lying to benefit the listener. This is the "Does this make me look fat?" type of lie. In addition to telling us to speak truthfully, God also tells us to encourage one another, especially those who are weak or timid. Sometimes the truth can hurt or discourage. The best advice here is probably what your mother told you. If you can't say something nice, don't say anything at all. But if you are asked, there is an alternative rather than lying; equivocation. "How do you like my new hairstyle?" "It's really you." Or "It's so unique and different." Equivocal statements can be understood in more than one way. They don't really say anything. And they are perfect for this type of situation. But if equivocation won't work, and the truth will be hurtful and not helpful, then I would opt for encouragement instead.

Seventh, lying to benefit a third party. This is Rahab's type of lie. When she lied, she had nothing to gain. She did gain later, but at the time, she didn't know what would happen. She could have been caught and killed. She was lying to protect the innocent. Corrie ten Boom and her family did the same thing for the Jews during the Holocaust. If you have nothing to gain, and your lie is to protect the innocent from harm, then I think God will honor it.

What about false prophets and teachers? Where do they fall in this scheme of things? Probably in category five, lying to gain power. False teachers can worm their way into any church and any congregation. We are easy prey for them, because we like what they tell us, since they tell us what we want to hear. But as Christ warned us, they appear in sheep's clothing, but inwardly they are ferocious wolves. They do not have our best interests at heart. They are concerned only for themselves. Worst of all, they have no concern for the truth of God. They are following their real father, the devil, who is the father of lies.

So what conclusions can we come to? Any lie told for our own benefit is wrong. We are to seek the approval of God rather than the approval of men. Any lie told in order to harm others is wrong. We are to treat others as we would want to be treated, and we are to be just and fair in our dealings with others. However, if we are faced with the situation of telling the truth and endangering innocent life, or lying and protecting that life, then I think God will honor our decision to withhold the truth. And in those cases where the truth will hurt rather than help, we must use our best judgment as to what we should say or do.

The question to ask ourselves is this: In my everyday life, am I generally truthful? Can my word be trusted? God is opposed to those who have a lifestyle of lying. We must examine our hearts to make sure our motives are pure before God, in our speech, and in all of our actions.

LESSON 12
THE TENTH COMMANDMENT: YOU SHALL NOT COVET.

Question 79: Which is the Tenth Commandment?

Answer: The Tenth Commandment is, "You shall not covet your neighbor's house; you shall not covet your neighbor's wife, or his male servant, or his female servant, or his ox, or his donkey, or anything that is your neighbor's."

1. What does "covet" mean?
   Read Deuteronomy 7:25; Micah 2:2 (You may also want to consult a good dictionary.)

Question 80: What is required in the Tenth Commandment?

Answer: The Tenth Commandment requires full contentment with our own condition, with a right and charitable frame of spirit toward our neighbor and all that is his.

2. What does it mean to have full contentment with our condition?
   Read Philippians 4:11-12; 1 Timothy 6:8

3. How can we accomplish that kind of contentment?
   Read Hebrews 13:5

Question 81: What is forbidden in the Tenth Commandment?

Answer: The Tenth Commandment forbids all discontentment with our own estate, envying or grieving at the good of our neighbor, and all unreasonable motions and affections toward anything that is his.

4. How does the Bible describe people who envy and covet what others have?
   Read Micah 2:1-2

5. How are our needs provided for?
   Read Matthew 6:8, 31-33

6. Does God only give us the basic necessities of life?
   Read Luke 11:13; Ephesians 3:20

7. What is the end result of covetousness and envy?
   Read James 4:2-3; Proverbs 14:30; Titus 3:3

8. What is the end result of working hard so we can have what our neighbors have?
   Read Ecclesiastes 4:4

9. What should our attitude be towards our neighbors?
   Read Philippians 2:3

10. What should we do if we need something that we cannot afford?
    Read Luke 11:9; 1 John 5:13-15

11. What things are you coveting that you need to let go?

LESSON 12
THE TENTH COMMANDMENT: YOU SHALL NOT COVET.

Catechism Questions 79, 80, and 81

I LIKE JEWELRY. I REALLY, REALLY LIKE JEWELRY. I BUY STERLING SILVER JEWelry because I like the color silver more than the color gold, and also because it is cheaper than gold and I can buy more of it. I have bought several pieces of jewelry from a certain shopping channel on television. My co-worker Alison also really likes jewelry, and she buys from that same shopping channel. At lunch one day, I was talking with Alison about that channel and I mentioned that I had seen a pair of earrings that I really liked, but I told her I had not bought them because I decided I didn't need them. She stopped eating, looked me straight in the eye, and said, "Paula. We don't need any of the jewelry we already have, much less any more jewelry."

No kidding. I could live my entire life without one piece of jewelry. It is certainly not a necessity. So when does my love of jewelry turn into covetousness? What exactly is covetousness? Dictionary.com gives its first definition of the word *covet*: "to desire wrongfully, inordinately, or without due regard for the rights of others." This would involve wanting what someone else has; not another one like it, but the exact thing they have. As the second definition, we are given: to wish for, esp. eagerly. This can be wrong, but it can be a good thing, depending on what we are coveting. (We'll get to that later.) The third definition is: to have an inordinate or wrongful desire. This desire could be for anything, whether it belongs to your neighbor or not.

Let's take each of these definitions and see how they might affect us. First, to desire wrongfully without regard for the rights of others, to want what others have. What does this lead to? At the very least, it leads to envy; why do they get to have that and I don't? At the very worst, it leads to murder. Look at the example of David and Bathsheba. What was the first sin David committed? It was actually lust. He saw Bathsheba and lusted after her. This led really quickly to coveting; he wanted her. So he took her, which was adultery. When the affair led to a baby, he called for her husband to come home from war, assuming that he would sleep with his wife and then think the baby was his. The plan was to get out of the mess by lying. But her husband would not indulge in those pleasures when the other soldiers were still at war. In the end, to save his reputation, David had Bathsheba's husband killed by military maneuvering. He resorted to murder. How many of the commandments did he break in this one event?

Does this kind of thing happen today? Of course it does. We hear about people murdering others for insurance money, for property, or even for a pair of expensive tennis shoes. But you are probably thinking, I might want something someone has, but I certainly wouldn't murder them for it. So let's look at definition two: to wish for eagerly.

Wishing for something is not necessarily wrong. In 1 Corinthians 12, in the King James version of the Bible, we are told to covet the greater spiritual gifts. More modern translations use the word desire, rather than covet, but it really means the same thing. If we are eagerly desiring the glory of God, or the prayers of others when we are in a difficult situation, or the wisdom to know how God is leading us, these things are not wrong. We are told to desire and seek these things. But if we are wishing for something to satisfy our own longings, we can be heading down the road to definition three: to have an inordinate or wrongful desire.

Why is it wrong to want something that much? Because it can take God's place in our lives. In Colossians 3:5, Paul tells us that greed, or covetousness, is the same thing as idolatry. We give first priority in our lives to the thing we are coveting; but first priority always belongs to God. By breaking the Tenth Commandment, we have come full circle back to breaking the First one.

So how are we to live? Very simply, we are to be content with what God has given us. When children are little, and even when they are a little older, they ask for things that their parents know they should not have. If a four-year-old wants to play with a butcher knife, will you let him? If a ten-year-old wants to drive to the grocery store, does she get the keys to the car? Of course not. We know that children at those ages are not ready for those responsibilities. In the same way, God knows what gifts and what responsibilities we are ready to handle. He gives us what we need, and He gives us what we can handle. He will not give us gifts that we will only use to further our sins. For example, if we have a tendency to be greedy and selfish, He will probably not give us more money just so we can spend it on ourselves.

Now, if you don't have a lot of money, I am not accusing you of being greedy and selfish. There are other reasons God may not give us certain things. My husband and I have had the "pleasure" of being in need and we know how hard that is. But we learned through those times how faithful God is. We have also had the pleasure of having more than enough to meet our needs, but we know that we cannot depend on our jobs or our bank accounts in the long run. We must always remember that all of our resources come from God alone.

One of the biggest problems in our society today is consumer debt. Where does that debt come from? From all of us wanting more than we can afford. Eventually that debt comes back to bite us. Proverbs 22:7 tells us that the rich rule over the poor, that the borrower is a servant of the lender. These two things are connected. The rich rule over the poor because the poor owe them money. The poor have borrowed from the rich and must now pay them back with interest. If you are in a position of debt, there are some great programs and books that can help you get out of debt. It will take work, but it will be worth it.

But what if our friends and neighbors have more than we have? How should we handle that? We should be humble and realize that God has given those things to them (or that they have accumulated a lot of debt and have more problems than we are even aware of). We should not be envious of their possessions or their lifestyle. We should focus on the things God has given us and not the things He hasn't. If you have a lot of trouble with this, look at some pictures of people in refugee camps, then make a list of everything you have that they don't. You will need more than one sheet of paper.

Finally, those who have been blessed and have plenty need to be careful of their attitude towards possessions. If you have wealth, do you flaunt your possessions? Do you talk about what you have bought, where you have been, or what you have inherited? Don't take pride in your possessions. They can go in an instant. Instead, make sure that your treasure is in heaven because that can never be destroyed. Be considerate of those who don't have what you have.

My church has a women's retreat every year and the cost to attend is minimal. But even that cost is too much for some of the women, so the retreat organizers wisely instituted a scholarship fund. Those who have resources can contribute to the fund, and those who have less can discreetly request a scholarship. No one but the scholarship committee knows who paid and who is on scholarship. In my opinion, there should never be a church function that is financially out of reach for anyone who wants to attend. And we must remember that what is a reasonable cost to some may be an exorbitant amount to others. My husband and I once had only ten dollars to buy food for two weeks. There may be people in your church in a similar situation.

Covetousness is a sin that can lead to many other sins. It is a sneaky thing that can creep up on us until it consumes our lives. We must constantly be on guard to make sure that nothing, absolutely nothing, takes the place in our lives that God should have. We must be content and at peace with the blessings God has given us, and we must not envy the things He gives our neighbors.

ABOUT THE AUTHOR

PAULA RODRIGUEZ IS THE WIFE OF PASTOR CHARLIE RODriguez and the mother of three daughters. In her life as the wife of a seminary student annd pastor, she has been privileged to live in two "seminary cities," where she has been able to sit under the teaching of some of the country's best theologians. She is also a teacher herself and has taught students of all ages, from pre-school through college, including a brief stint as a home-school mom. She has a graduate degree in Communication and is currently the Chair of the Speech, Theatre, and Dance Department at Hinds Community College in Mississippi. She is an accomplished speaker and has been a Bible Study leader for many years.

www.ingramcontent.com/pod-product-compliance
Lightning Source LLC
LaVergne TN
LVHW021407080426
835508LV00020B/2477